LAWYER'S WIT AND WISDOM

Other books in this series:

L A W Y E R ' S   W I T   A N D   W I S D O M

Quotations on the Legal Profession, In Brief

Edited by Bruce Nash and Allan Zullo
Compiled by Kathryn Zullo

RUNNING PRESS
PHILADELPHIA · LONDON

9 8

Digit on the right indicates the number of this printing.

Library of Congress Cataloging-in-Publication number 94–73880

ISBN 1–56138–650–2

Cover design by Toby Schmidt
Cover illustration by William Waitzman
Interior design by Paul Kepple
Interior illustrations by Tim Lewis
Edited by William King
Printed in the United States of America.

This book may be ordered by mail from the publisher.
Please add $2.50 for postage and handling.
But try your bookstore first!

Running Press Book Publishers
125 South Twenty-second Street
Philadelphia, Pennsylvania 19103–4399

CONTENTS

A C K N O W L E D G E M E N T S

The authors wish to thank the American Bar Association
for its cooperation in allowing us to adapt many of the anecdotes
in this book from two of its publications.

Several anecdotes were first reported in the monthly
"War Stories" feature in the *ABA Journal*, which graciously
granted us permission to edit and reprint them.

Other anecdotes were adapted from an annual feature
called "Legal Lunacies" by Barbara Kate Repa, which appeared
between 1985 and 1993 in *Student Lawyer* magazine, also published by
the American Bar Association. *Student Lawyer* granted us permission
to edit and reprint these items, for which we are grateful.

NO GROUP IS EXALTED OR VILIFIED MORE THAN LAWYERS. IN SHAKESPEARE'S <u>HENRY VI</u>, PART II, ACT IV, DICK THE BUTCHER FANTASIZES: "THE FIRST THING WE DO, LET'S KILL ALL THE LAWYERS"—PROBABLY THE WORLD'S FAVORITE QUOTE REGARDING THE PROFESSION. BUT BEFORE DICK'S SYMPATHIZERS JUDGE TOO QUICKLY, THEY SHOULD AT LEAST WEIGH THE TESTIMONY OF WELL-KNOWN DEFENSE ATTORNEY ELLIS RUBIN: "BEING A LAWYER IS ABOUT SERVING JUSTICE. THAT'S NOT ONLY OUR GREATEST CALLING, IT'S OUR ONLY CALLING."

THE LEGAL PROFESSION TRIGGERS DIVERSE OPINIONS AND FEELINGS BECAUSE LAWYERS DEAL WITH EXTREMES OF THE HUMAN CONDITION, USUALLY INTERACTING WITH PEOPLE IN TIMES OF GREAT NEED AND STRESS. AS FAMED JURIST OLIVER WENDELL HOLMES JR. ONCE SAID, "IN WHAT OTHER [PROFESSION]

DOES ONE PLUNGE SO DEEP IN THE STREAM OF LIFE, SO SHARE ITS PASSIONS, ITS BATTLES, ITS DESPAIR, ITS TRIUMPHS, BOTH AS WITNESS AND ACTOR?"

ALTHOUGH THE LAW HAS CHANGED OVER THE CENTURIES, THE RELATIONSHIP BETWEEN ATTORNEYS AND CLIENTS HAS REMAINED PRETTY MUCH THE SAME—IT'S STILL A LOVE-HATE AFFAIR. NO WONDER PEOPLE FROM ALL WALKS OF LIFE HAVE NEVER BEEN AT A LOSS FOR WORDS WHEN REVEALING THEIR TRUE FEELINGS ABOUT LAWYERS. IN THIS BOOK, THE QUOTATIONS RANGE FROM INSIGHTFUL AND PITHY QUOTES FROM FAMOUS JUDGES AND PHILOSOPHERS TO LIGHT-HEARTED QUIPS FROM FICTIONAL CHARACTERS AND SATIRISTS. AND SOMETIMES TRUTH IS STRANGER THAN FICTION, AS THE LEAVENING OF HUMOROUS TRUE-LIFE ANECDOTES ABOUT LIFE IN THE LEGAL WORLD PROVES.

WORDS HAVE BEEN—AND ALWAYS WILL BE—THE BASIC TOOLS OF THE LAWYER. SAID NOTED LEGAL SCHOLAR CHARLES ALAN WRIGHT, "WHETHER WE ARE TRYING A CASE, WRITING A BRIEF, DRAFTING A CONTRACT, OR NEGOTIATING WITH AN ADVERSARY, WORDS ARE THE ONLY THINGS WE HAVE TO WORK WITH."

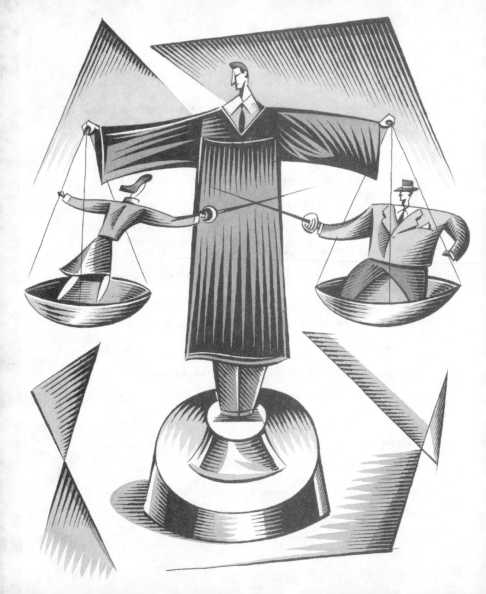

THE PEOPLE

Common sense often makes a good law.

WILLIAM O. DOUGLAS,
SUPREME COURT JUSTICE

If you like laws and sausages, you should never
watch either one being made.

OTTO VON BISMARCK,
19TH-CENTURY PRUSSIAN PRINCE

The law is like the killy-loo bird, a creature
that insisted on flying backward because it
didn't care where it was going but was mightily
interested where it had been.

FRED RODELL,
LAW PROFESSOR, YALE UNIVERSITY

All laws are an attempt to domesticate the
natural ferocity of the species.

JOHN W. GARDNER,
U.S. SECRETARY OF HEALTH, EDUCATION,
AND WELFARE

Law is born from despair of human nature.

JOSE ORTEGA Y GASSET,
19TH-CENTURY SPANISH PHILOSOPHER

16

The laws sometimes sleep, but never die.

ANONYMOUS

The law, in its majesty equality, forbids all men
to sleep under bridges, to beg in the streets,
and to steal bread—the rich as well as the poor.

ANATOLE FRANCE,
FRENCH WRITER

The wording of laws should mean the same thing to all men.

CHARLES LOUIS DE MONTESQUIEU, 17TH-CENTURY FRENCH LAWYER AND POLITICAL PHILOSOPHER

Laws are felt only when the individual comes into conflict with them.

SUZANNE LA FOLLETTE, AMERICAN POLITICIAN AND FEMINIST

Where-ever Law ends, Tyranny begins.

JOHN LOCKE, 17TH-CENTURY ENGLISH PHILOSOPHER

Law is a pledge that the citizens of a state will do justice to one another.

LYCOPHRON, 3RD-CENTURY B.C. GREEK POET AND SCHOLAR

The law: It has honored us; may we honor it.

DANIEL WEBSTER,
18TH-CENTURY AMERICAN STATESMAN,
ORATOR, AND LAWYER

If we desire respect for the law we must first
make the law respectable.

LOUIS D. BRANDEIS,
SUPREME COURT JUSTICE

Good laws lead to the making of better ones;
bad ones bring about worse.

JEAN JACQUES ROUSSEAU,
18TH-CENTURY FRENCH PHILOSOPHER AND WRITER

Riches without law are more dangerous than
is poverty without law.

HENRY WARD BEECHER,
19TH-CENTURY AMERICAN CLERGYMAN

I say that you cannot administer a wicked law impartially. You can only destroy. You can only punish. I warn you that a wicked law, like cholera, destroys everyone it touches—its upholders as well as its defiers.

**SPENCER TRACY AS HENRY DRUMMOND
IN THE FILM INHERIT THE WIND**

Nothing is more destructive of respect for the government and the law of the land than passing laws which cannot be enforced.

**ALBERT EINSTEIN,
GERMAN-BORN AMERICAN PHYSICIST**

It may be true that the law cannot make a man love me, but it can keep him from lynching me, and I think that's pretty important.

**DR. MARTIN LUTHER KING JR.,
AMERICAN CLERGYMAN
AND CIVIL RIGHTS LEADER**

Whereas the law is passionless, passion must
never sway the heart of man.

**ARISTOTLE,
4TH-CENTURY B.C. GREEK PHILOSOPHER**

Law is a Bottomless-Pit, it is a Cormorant,
a Harpy, that devours every thing.

**JOHN ARBUTHNOT,
17TH-CENTURY SCOTTISH PHYSICIAN AND WRITER**

Law: an ordinance of reason for the common good,
made by him who has care of the community.

**ST. THOMAS AQUINAS,
13TH-CENTURY ITALIAN THEOLOGIAN**

The good of the people is the supreme law.

**CICERO,
2ND-CENTURY B.C. ROMAN STATESMAN,
ORATOR, AND WRITER**

Law is a formless mass of isolated decisions.

MORRIS COHEN,
RUSSIAN-BORN AMERICAN PHILOSOPHER

Laws should be like clothes. They should be made
to fit the people they are meant to serve.

CLARENCE DARROW,
AMERICAN LAWYER AND WRITER

Law is order, and good law is good order.

ARISTOTLE,
4TH-CENTURY B.C. GREEK PHILOSOPHER

The law is a sort of hocus-pocus science that smiles
in yer face while it picks yer pocket.

CHARLES MACKLIN,
17TH-CENTURY IRISH ACTOR AND DRAMATIST

Law and order are always and everywhere the
law and order which protect the
established hierarchy.

HERBERT MARCUSE,
GERMAN-BORN AMERICAN PHILOSOPHER

Men have feelings but the law does not.

NAPOLEON I,
EMPEROR OF FRANCE

Law is a majestic edifice, sheltering all of us,
each stone of which rests on another.

JOHN GALSWORTHY,
ENGLISH WRITER AND DRAMATIST

The law is the true embodiment of
everything that's excellent.

WILLIAM S. GILBERT,
ENGLISH POET AND WRITER

A law can be both economic folly
and constitutional.

ANTONIN SCALIA,
SUPREME COURT JUSTICE

Law is the harmony of the world.

RICHARD HOOKER,
16TH-CENTURY ENGLISH THEOLOGIAN

The law is so phallic! It doesn't leave much
room for sensitivity, which must be why so
many guys are happy in it.

ALYSON SINGER,
AMERICAN LAWYER

23

Law is experience developed by reason
and applied continually to further experience.

ROSCOE POUND,
DEAN EMERITUS, HARVARD LAW SCHOOL

The law is not majestic. The law is what public opinion says it is. I could tell you a lot about the law. . . . We got a man to argue for me tomorrow who wouldn't have me to dinner in his house. He talks on the phone with the President. But I have paid his price and he will be at my side for as long as it takes.

DUTCH SCHULTZ,
NOTORIOUS DEPRESSION-ERA MOBSTER,
IN E. L. DOCTOROW'S BILLY BATHGATE

24

The Law is good, if a man use it lawfully.

I TIMOTHY, 1:8

Law is the backbone which keeps man erect.

S. C. YUTER,
AMERICAN JOURNALIST AND WRITER

Law is but a heathen word for power.

DANIEL DEFOE,
17TH-CENTURY ENGLISH WRITER

The law is reason free from passion.

ARISTOTLE,
4TH-CENTURY B.C. GREEK PHILOSOPHER

The law will never make men free;
it is men who have got to make the law free.

HENRY DAVID THOREAU,
19TH-CENTURY AMERICAN WRITER

The more laws, the more offenders.

THOMAS FULLER,
17TH-CENTURY ENGLISH WRITER

The laws of a nation form the most instructive
portion of its history.

**EDWARD GIBBON,
18TH-CENTURY ENGLISH HISTORIAN**

Woman throughout the ages has been mistress
to the law, as man has been its master.

**FREDA ADLER,
AMERICAN EDUCATOR**

The law sees and treats women the
way men see and treat women.

**CATHARINE MACKINNON,
AMERICAN LAW PROFESSOR, FEMINIST, AND WRITER**

It usually takes a hundred years to make a law,
and then, after it has done its work, it usually takes
a hundred years to get rid of it.

**HENRY WARD BEECHER,
19TH-CENTURY AMERICAN CLERGYMAN**

The law can never make us as secure
as we are when we do not need it.

ALEXANDER M. BICKEL,
ROMANIAN-BORN AMERICAN LEGAL SCHOLAR

The criminal law represents the pathology of civilization.

MORRIS COHEN,
RUSSIAN-BORN AMERICAN PHILOSOPHER

Laws too gentle are seldom obeyed;
too severe, seldom executed.

BENJAMIN FRANKLIN,
18TH-CENTURY AMERICAN STATESMAN
AND PHILOSOPHER

I know no method to secure the repeal of
bad or obnoxious laws so effective as
their stringent execution.

ULYSSES S. GRANT,
18TH PRESIDENT OF THE UNITED STATES

A strict observance of the written laws is
doubtless one of the high virtues of a good citizen,
but it is not the highest. The laws of necessity,
of self-preservation, of saving our country
when in danger, are of higher obligation.

**THOMAS JEFFERSON,
3RD PRESIDENT OF THE UNITED STATES**

It is difficult to make our material condition
better by the best laws, but it is easy
enough to ruin it by bad laws.

**THEODORE ROOSEVELT,
26TH PRESIDENT OF THE UNITED STATES**

Many laws as certainly make bad men,
as bad men make many laws.

**WALTER SAVAGE LANDOR,
18TH-CENTURY ENGLISH WRITER**

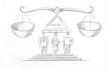

Moral principle is the foundation of law.

**RONALD D. DWORKIN,
LAW PROFESSOR, NEW YORK UNIVERSITY**

A multitude of laws in a country is like
a great number of physicians;
a sign of weakness and malady.

**VOLTAIRE,
18TH-CENTURY FRENCH WRITER**

The best law leaves the least discretion
to the judge.

LATIN PROVERB

The laws put the safety of all
above the safety of one.

**CICERO,
2ND-CENTURY B.C. ROMAN STATESMAN,
ORATOR, AND WRITER**

The purpose of law is to prevent the strong
from always having their way.

OVID,
1ST-CENTURY ROMAN POET

As physicians are the preservers of the sick,
so are the laws of the injured.

EPICTETUS,
4TH-CENTURY B.C. GREEK PHILOSOPHER

Every law which originated in ignorance
and malice, and gratifies the passions from which
it sprang, we call the wisdom of our ancestors.

SYDNEY SMITH,
19TH-CENTURY ENGLISH WRITER

Laws are inherited like diseases.

JOHANN WOLFGANG VON GOETHE,
18TH-CENTURY GERMAN POET AND DRAMATIST

No laws, however stringent, can make the idle industrious,
the thriftless provident, or the drunken sober.

SAMUEL SMILES,
19TH-CENTURY ENGLISH WRITER

Men would be great criminals did they need
as many laws as they make.

LORD C. J. DARLING,
19TH-CENTURY ENGLISH JUDGE

31

When men are pure, laws are useless; when
men are corrupt, laws are broken.

BENJAMIN DISRAELI,
19TH-CENTURY BRITISH PRIME MINISTER

Someone has tabulated that we have 35
million laws on the books to enforce
the ten commandments.

BERT MASTERSON

Laws are spider webs; they hold the weak
and delicate who are caught in their meshes,
but are torn in pieces by the rich and powerful.

ANACHARSIS,
1ST-CENTURY B.C. SCYTHIAN PHILOSOPHER

Law is certain in meaning, just in precept,
convenient in execution, agreeable to the form
of government, and productive of virtue
in those that live under it.

FRANCIS BACON,
16TH-CENTURY ENGLISH PHILOSOPHER
AND WRITER

32

Laws are not made for a righteous man,
but for the lawless and disobedient,
for the ungodly and for sinners.

I TIMOTHY, 1: 9

Postulating on the Predominating
Principles of Pollution

In his opinion in a 1974 case involving the dumping of garbage in an unauthorized area, Georgia Appellate Judge H. Sol Banks proved he was an avid alliterationist. He wrote:

"Preventing public pollution permits promiscuous perusal of personalty but persistent perspicacious patron persuasively provided pertinent perdurable preponderating presumption precedent preventing prison."

In other words, the defendant was found not guilty.

33

When No Means No

In a 1973 decision involving school segregation in Denver, Supreme Court Justice William J. Brennan Jr. achieved great notoriety among fellow jurists. It wasn't for his opinion, but for his penning of the Court's first quadruple negative sentence. He wrote:

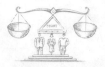

"This is not to say, however, that the prima facie case may not be met by evidence supporting a finding that a lesser degree of segregated schooling in the core city area would not have resulted even if the Board had not acted as it did."

A Great Judge of Weather

Samuel King, a U.S. District Court Judge in California, was annoyed that bad weather was keeping people from showing up for jury duty.

On February 18, 1986, he decreed: "I hereby order that it cease raining by Tuesday." California then suffered five years of drought.

So in 1991, he issued another decree: "I hereby rescind my order of February 18, 1986, and order that rain shall fall in California beginning February 27, 1991."

Days later, the state was hit by its heaviest rains in 10 years.

From Here to Eternity

A lease offered by a South Florida shopping center developer contains the following "End of the World" clause:

"If the end of the world is imminent before all Tenant's obligations are fully performed, then Landlord may elect to declare all rents to the end of the term to be immediately due and payable in full and may be enforced against Tenant by any available procedure. For remedial purposes, Landlord will be deemed aligned with the forces of light, and Tenant with forces of darkness, regardless of the parties' actual ultimate destinations, unless and until Landlord elects otherwise in writing."

L A W Y E R S

A lawyer's relationship to justice and wisdom . . .
is on a par with a piano tuner's relationship to a
concert. He neither composes the music, nor interprets
it—he merely keeps the machinery running.

LUCILLE KALLEN,
20TH-CENTURY WRITER

Lawyers are . . . operators of the toll bridge across which
anyone in search of justice must pass.

JANE BRYANT QUINN,
AMERICAN JOURNALIST

Being a lawyer is about serving justice. That's not only
our greatest calling, it's our only calling.

ELLIS RUBIN,
AMERICAN LAWYER

The lawyer's job in practice is to be on one hand
the impassioned representative of his client to
the world, and on the other the wise representative
to his client of the legal system and the society,
explaining and upholding the demands and
restrictions that system places on them both.

SCOTT TUROW,
AMERICAN LAWYER AND WRITER

To be an effective criminal defense counsel,
an attorney must be prepared to be demanding,
outrageous, irreverent, blasphemous, a rogue, a renegade,
and a hated, isolated and lonely person. . . .
few love a spokesman for the despised and the damned.

CLARENCE DARROW,
AMERICAN LAWYER AND WRITER

37

Most good lawyers live well, work hard, and die poor.

DANIEL WEBSTER,
18TH-CENTURY AMERICAN STATESMAN, ORATOR, AND LAWYER

A personal injury lawyer is in a position to level
the playing field and help people under our legal system.

PHILIP CORBOY,
AMERICAN LAWYER

The trial lawyer does what Socrates was executed for:
making the worse argument appear the stronger.

IRVING R. KAUFMAN,
U.S. COURT OF APPEALS JUDGE

Law is a profession which abounds with honorable men,
and in which there are fewer scamps than in any other.

GEORGE BORROW,
19TH-CENTURY ENGLISH WRITER AND LINGUIST

A lawyer without history or literature is a mechanic,
a mere working mason.

SIR WALTER SCOTT,
18TH-CENTURY SCOTTISH POET AND WRITER

A good lawyer has a grasp of what yesterday teaches us about today and tomorrow, and knows that the real meaning of words like "freedom" or "justice" can only be found in the tapestry of history.

SOL M. LINOWITZ,
AMERICAN LAWYER

Anyone who believes a better day dawns when lawyers are eliminated bears the burden of explaining who will take their place. Who will protect the poor, the injured, the victims of negligence, the victims of racial discrimination and the victims of racial violence?

JOHN J. CURTIN JR.,
AMERICAN LAWYER

I've never met a litigator who didn't think he was winning—right up until the moment the guillotine dropped.

WILLIAM F. BAXTER,
ASSISTANT U.S. ATTORNEY GENERAL

You cannot live without the lawyers,
and certainly you cannot die without them.

JOSEPH H. CHOATE,
AMERICAN LAWYER AND DIPLOMAT

A lawyer is a learned gentleman who rescues
your estate from your enemies and keeps it himself.

LORD HENRY PETER BROUGHAM,
18TH-CENTURY SCOTTISH JUDGE AND POLITICAL LEADER

I am not so afraid of lawyers as I used to be.
They are lambs in wolves' clothing.

EDNA ST. VINCENT MILLAY,
AMERICAN POET

The animals are not as stupid as one thinks—
they have neither doctors nor lawyers.

L. DOCQUIER,
FRENCH APHORIST

My daddy is a movie actor, and sometimes he plays the
good guy, and sometimes he plays the lawyer.

MALCOLM FORD,
ON WHAT HIS FATHER, ACTOR HARRISON
FORD, DOES FOR A LIVING

Show me your briefs and I'll show you mine.

PLJ,
SEEKING "AN ATTRACTIVE,
SLIM & WITTY SINGLE
WHITE FEMALE LAWYER, 25–30,
FOR 'COURT-SHIP,'" THROUGH
"PERSONALS FOR PROFESSIONALS"
IN THE NEW YORK LAW JOURNAL

Lawyers like to throw around jargon and
flowery language because it makes them feel
self-important and prestigious.

GEORGE HATHAWAY,
AMERICAN WRITER

I don't know of any other industry,
except the movie business, that has so many stars.
Every lawyer thinks he's special.

PETER MORRISON,
AMERICAN LAWYER

No splints yet invented will heal a lawyer's broken reputation.

PAUL O'NEIL,
AMERICAN JOURNALIST AND WRITER

42

You want the unvarnished and ungarnished truth,
and I'm no hand for that. I'm a lawyer.

MARY ROBERTS RINEHART,
AMERICAN WRITER

The New England folks have a saying,
that three Philadelphia lawyers are a match
for the very devil himself.

SALEM OBSERVER

Lawyers take to politics like bears take to honey.

ROBERT TOWNSEND,
AMERICAN BUSINESSMAN

A peasant between two lawyers is like a fish between two cats.

SPANISH PROVERB

What chance has the ignorant, uncultivated liar against the
educated expert? What chance have I . . . against a lawyer?

MARK TWAIN,
AMERICAN WRITER AND HUMORIST

43

I have a high opinion of lawyers. With all their faults,
they stack up well against those in every other occupation
or profession. They are better to work with or play
with or fight with or drink with than most
other varieties of mankind.

HARRISON TWEED,
AMERICAN LAWYER

A lawyer with a briefcase can steal more than
a hundred men with guns.

**DON CORLEONE
IN MARIO PUZO'S THE GODFATHER**

I think we may class the lawyer in the
natural history of monsters.

**JOHN KEATS,
18TH-CENTURY ENGLISH POET**

The best description of "utter waste" would be a busload
of lawyers to go over a cliff with three empty seats.

**LAMAR HUNT,
OWNER, KANSAS CITY CHIEFS FOOTBALL TEAM**

Young lawyers attend the courts, not because
they have business there but because they have
no business anywhere else.

**WASHINGTON IRVING,
18TH-CENTURY AMERICAN WRITER**

Why is there always a secret singing when a lawyer
cashes in? Why does a hearse horse
snicker hauling a lawyer away?

CARL SANDBURG,
AMERICAN WRITER

Lawyer: The only man in whom ignorance
of the law is not punished.

ELBERT HUBBARD,
AMERICAN WRITER AND EDITOR

A lawyer's job is to manipulate the skeletons
in other people's closets.

SOL STEIN,
AMERICAN BUSINESSMAN AND WRITER

When God wanted to chastise mankind,
He invented lawyers.

RUSSIAN PROVERB

A lawyer's dream of heaven—every man reclaimed
his property at the resurrection, and each tried to
recover it from all his forefathers.

SAMUEL BUTLER,
19TH-CENTURY ENGLISH JOURNALIST AND WRITER

When there's a rift in the lute, the business of the
lawyer is to widen the rift and gather the loot.

ARTHUR HAYS,
AMERICAN LAWYER

Lawyers use the law as shoemakers use leather:
rubbing it, pressing it, and stretching it
with their teeth, all to the end of making it
fit for their purposes.

LOUIS XII,
KING OF FRANCE

If you can think of something which is connected with something without thinking of the something it is connected to, you have a legal mind.

**THOMAS REED POWELL,
PROFESSOR, HARVARD UNIVERSITY**

Some people think that a lawyer's business is to make white black; but his real business is to make white in spite of the stained and soiled condition which renders its true color questionable. He is simply an intellectual washing machine.

**LOGAN E. BLECKLEY,
AMERICAN JUDGE**

47

Lawyers are always more ready to get a man into troubles than out of them.

**OLIVER GOLDSMITH,
18TH-CENTURY ENGLISH WRITER**

God works wonders now and then. Behold:
a lawyer, an honest man.

**BENJAMIN FRANKLIN,
18TH-CENTURY AMERICAN STATESMAN
AND PHILOSOPHER**

Only painters and lawyers can change white to black.

JAPANESE PROVERB

No lawyer will ever go to Heaven so long
as there is room for more in Hell.

FRENCH PROVERB

Lawyers and soldiers are the Devil's playmates.

FRENCH PROVERB

The Devil makes his Christmas pie of lawyers' tongues.

ENGLISH PROVERB

Lawyers, like bread, [are best] when they are young and new.

THOMAS FULLER,
17TH-CENTURY ENGLISH CLERGYMAN AND WRITER

A man without money needs no more fear a crowd
of lawyers than a crowd of pickpockets.

WILLIAM WYCHERLEY,
17TH-CENTURY ENGLISH WRITER

He saw a lawyer killing a viper
On a dunghill hard by his own stable,
And the Devil smiled, for it put him in mind
Of Cain and his brother Abel.

SAMUEL TAYLOR COLERIDGE,
18TH-CENTURY ENGLISH POET

49

A barrister of extended practice, if he has any
talents at all, is the best companion in the world.

SIR WALTER SCOTT,
18TH-CENTURY SCOTTISH POET AND WRITER

It is a horrible demoralizing thing to be a lawyer. You look for such low motives in everyone and everything.

KATHERINE T. HINKSON,
IRISH POET AND WRITER

The bar is still dominated by shortsightedness and self-interest. Spotting change there is like watching a glacier move.

VERNON COUNTRYMAN,
PROFESSOR, HARVARD UNIVERSITY

50

Most lawyers are like whores. They serve the client who puts the highest fee on the table.

FLORYNCE RAE KENNEDY,
AMERICAN LAWYER AND CIVIL RIGHTS ACTIVIST

A lot of defense attorneys take the facts of the case and twist them around and try, in effect, to create a lie out of some truth.

JOHN KATZENBACH,
AMERICAN JOURNALIST

Attorneys are just good followers. . . .
The lawyer mentality is to follow the rules
and make a big pile doing it.

HARRY PALMER,
AMERICAN LAWYER

We are more casual about qualifying the people
we allow to act as advocates in the courtroom than
we are about licensing electricians.

WARREN BURGER,
SUPREME COURT JUSTICE

Most lawyers, it seems to me, simply can't balance
their energies: the goal of success and more
money chips away at them until they have succumbed
to a dangerous kind of myopia.

H. JAMES THOMAS,
AMERICAN LAWYER

Heaven Help Them

Attorney Rodney Donohoo, of Santa Ana, California, was riding up an elevator with two elderly women one day in 1990. One of the ladies asked if lawyers had offices on all the top floors of the building.

"Yes, they do," Donohoo replied.

"It's a good thing," the woman told her friend. "That's probably as close to heaven as most lawyers will ever get."

A Fool For a Client

In a 1985 criminal trial, Michael Blackwell, of Bridgeport, Connecticut, represented himself. At the end of the two-day trial, he was found guilty of two counts of attempted robbery by a jury that took less than a hour to deliberate.

As soon as the verdict was read, Blackwell told the judge he planned to appeal. When the judged asked him on what grounds, Blackwell replied, "I had an incompetent defense."

If At First You Don't Succeed . . .

In 1967, Maxcy Filer, then 36 years old and fresh out of law school, took the California bar exam for the first time.

He flunked the grueling three-day test. So he tried again . . . and again . . . and again. Twenty-four frustrating years later, Filer finally passed—on his 47th try, at the age of 60.

"I never once thought seriously about giving up," he said.

What Gave Me Away?

Convicted con man Peter Horsford, who was accused of impersonating a lawyer, had trouble getting a trial date in New York in 1988.

The problem was that four of the judges considered for his trial were disqualified from hearing the case—because he had argued cases in their courtrooms.

"I should have suspected he wasn't a lawyer," said one of the judges. "He was always so punctual and polite."

Legal Briefs

Miami lawyer Alvin Goodman showed up at the Metropolitan Correctional Center early one Sunday in 1989 to see a client. But because the attorney was violating the dress code by wearing shorts, he was denied entry.

Rather than go all the way home, Goodman stopped off at a nearby garage sale. Although there were no pants, he bought a nice turquoise skirt. He put it on and returned to the correctional center.

When the guard balked, Goodman argued that if women wearing pants are allowed inside, then men wearing skirts should be, too. The guard reluctantly agreed.

Two Sides to Everything

In the 1920s, a plaintiff brought suit against the City of New York after he claimed to have been seriously injured from falling into an open manhole.

During his trial, Dr. Willard Parker, appearing as an expert witness for the plaintiff, testified that the

plaintiff "had been so badly hurt that he could lie on only one side."

Whereupon the city attorney joked, "I suppose, doctor, you mean he would make a very poor lawyer?"

In the Name of Love

Seattle attorney Jeffrey Leppo was relieved when the judge granted his motion for a postponement of a case he was to argue in federal court in 1991.

But then to his shock, the lawyer realized that the new date of the trial fell during his honeymoon. So Leppo filed a motion for a second postponement. Without it, he feared, there might not even be a wedding, let alone a honeymoon. Said Leppo in his motion, "It has taken counsel over 34 years to find someone whom he loves and who loves him."

A sympathetic judge granted the motion, and Leppo's wedding went off without a hitch.

When Worlds Collide

In 1988, attorney Becky Klemt of Laramie, Wyoming, wrote letters to several attorneys in California offering a job to collect child support for a client whose husband had moved to Los Angeles.

In declining the offer, lawyer Stephen Corris, who specializes in international trade, wrote Klemt, "Without sounding pretentious, my current retainer for cases is a flat $100,000, with an additional charge of $1,000 an hour."

Klemt then fired off a letter back to Corris, saying in part, "Steve, I've got news—you can't say you charge a $100,000 retainer fee and an additional $1,000 an hour without sounding pretentious. It just can't be done. Especially when you're writing to someone in Laramie, Wyoming, where you're considered pretentious if you wear socks to court or drive anything fancier than a Ford Bronco. Hell, Steve, all the lawyers in Laramie, put together, don't charge $1,000 an hour. . . .

"P.S.: Incidentally, we have advised our client of your hourly rate. She is willing to pay you $1,000 per hour to collect this judgment, provided it doesn't take you more than four seconds."

CLIENTS

Client, n. A person who has made the
customary choice between the two methods
of being legally robbed.

AMBROSE BIERCE,
AMERICAN WRITER

If you're a litigating attorney, always discuss tactics
with the client at the trial. Not only will this
surprise your adversary but your client as well.

ARTHUR GREEBLER,
AMERICAN LAWYER

57

I'd rather have my hand cut off than betray
the interests of a client.

RAYMOND BURR
AS TELEVISION LAWYER PERRY MASON

Definition of a lawyer's function: To protect his clients from being persuaded by persons whom they do not know to enter into contracts which they do not understand to purchase goods which they do not want with money which they have not got.

LORD WILFRID ARTHUR GREENE,
ENGLISH JUDGE

Praise the adversary. He is the catalyst by which you bill your client. Damn the client.
He is your true enemy.

STEVEN J. KUMBLE,
AMERICAN LAWYER

About half the practice of a decent lawyer consists in telling would-be clients that they are damned fools and should stop.

ELIHU ROOT,
AMERICAN LAWYER AND STATESMAN

[The] ideal client is the very wealthy man
in very great trouble.

JOHN STERLING,
AMERICAN LAWYER

Don't try to instruct your lawyer.
If you do, you've got the wrong lawyer.

JOHN T. NOLAN

59

An investigation is underway, and for the first
time in my life I may actually have to stoop to retaining
a lawyer. This is the end of something pure and good.
Once a fellow breaks down and hires his first
attorney, he has gone and booked himself passage
aboard the hand basket to Hades.

TOM ROBBINS,
AMERICAN WRITER

Of course people are getting smarter nowadays;
they are letting lawyers instead of their
conscience be their guides.

**WILL ROGERS,
AMERICAN ACTOR AND HUMORIST**

If there is any truth to the old proverb that "one who
is his own lawyer has a fool for a client," the Court . . .
now bestows a constitutional right on one
to make a fool of himself.

**HARRY A. BLACKMUN,
SUPREME COURT JUSTICE, DISSENTING IN
A 6-3 RULING THAT ALLOWED A DEFENDANT
TO REFUSE COUNSEL**

Journalists are a hard group of people to love,
but they're an easy group to defend.

**FLOYD ABRAMS,
AMERICAN LAWYER**

Chutzpa is that quality enshrined in a man who, having killed his mother and father, throws himself on the mercy of the court because he is an orphan.

**LEO ROSTEN,
POLISH-AMERICAN WRITER**

A defendant is entitled to a fair trial but not a perfect one.

U.S. SUPREME COURT

If there were no bad people there would be no good lawyers.

**CHARLES DICKENS,
19TH-CENTURY ENGLISH WRITER**

There is never a deed so foul that something couldn't be said for the guy; that's why there are lawyers.

**MELVIN BELLI,
AMERICAN LAWYER**

Things in law tend to be black and white.
But we all know that some people are a little bit guilty,
while other people are guilty as hell.

DONALD R. CRESSEY,
AMERICAN WRITER

I don't know if I want a lawyer to tell me what
I cannot do. I hire him to tell me how to
do what I want to do.

J.P. MORGAN,
AMERICAN FINANCIER

I get paid for seeing that my clients have every
break the law allows. I have knowingly
defended a number of guilty men. But the guilty
never escape unscathed. My fees are sufficient
punishment for anyone.

F. LEE BAILEY,
AMERICAN LAWYER

In former days, everyone found the assumption
of innocence so easy; today we find fatally
easy the assumption of guilt.

AMANDA CROSS,
AMERICAN LITERARY SCHOLAR AND WRITER

A woman has a much better chance than a man
of acquittal on a murder charge. . . . If she happens to
be a blonde, her chances rise about 45 percent.

JOHN MCGEORGE,
AUSTRALIAN PSYCHIATRIST

Fools and obstinate men make lawyers rich.

HENRY GEORGE BOHN,
19TH-CENTURY ENGLISH PUBLISHER

It took man thousands of years to put words down on
paper, and his lawyers still wish he wouldn't.

MIGNON MCLAUGHLIN,
AMERICAN WRITER

He who is always his own counselor will often
have a fool for his client.

PORT FOLIO (A PHILADELPHIA MAGAZINE),
AUGUST 1809

Preemptive Justice

Years ago in Kentucky, a prosecutor offered to settle the charge in a criminal case if the defendant would plead guilty and accept a five-year sentence.

On the advice of his defense attorney, the defendant turned down the deal. The case went to trial, where he was eventually convicted. Before imposing a life sentence without parole, the judged asked the defendant if he had anything to say.

"Yes, your honor," said the defendant. "You might as well tack on a few more years—because if I ever get out, I'm gonna kill my lawyer!"

The Whole Truth and Nothing But

During a 1989 case in municipal court in Middletown, Ohio, a lawyer asked the judge to be excused from representing his client.

The judge scanned the courtroom, looking for a suitable replacement. But before he could find one, the defendant stood up and said, "That's all right, Judge. I won't be needing another lawyer. I've decided to tell the truth."

Once Bitten . . .

About a year after unsuccessfully defending a client, British lawyer Sir Patrick Hastings found himself cross-examining the very same man in another trial.

The witness was not being cooperative, so Sir Patrick, who did not realize the man was once his client, warned him, "You will answer my questions directly, take my advice."

"I will not take your advice, sir," the witness snapped. "I took it once and it put me inside [jail] for six months."

L A W   F I R M S

The screening process through which law firms
choose new partners is perhaps as well considered as
anything this side of a papal election.

**NEAL JOHNSTON,
CHIEF OF STAFF, NEW YORK CITY COUNCIL**

Panic is a way of life in a major law firm, and clients like
Sonny Capps can cause ulcers. Our clients are
our only assets, so we kill ourselves for them.

**LAWYER OLIVER LAMBERT,
IN JOHN GRISHAM'S THE FIRM**

No one is under pressure. There wasn't a light on
when I left at 2 o'clock this morning.

**HOYT MOONE,
AMERICAN LAWYER**

We shake papers at each other the way
primitive tribes shake spears.

JOHN JAY OSBORN JR.,
AUTHOR OF THE ASSOCIATES

I regret that I have but one law firm
to give to my country.

ADLAI E. STEVENSON,
AMERICAN LAWYER AND DIPLOMAT,
REFERRING TO PRESIDENT JOHN KENNEDY'S
REPEATED SELECTION OF MEMBERS OF
STEVENSON'S LAW FIRM TO SERVE IN
HIS ADMINISTRATION

To compensate for minor irregularities in
the earth's rotation, official international
timekeepers add one second to this day.
U.S. law firms adjust their bills.

DAVE BARRY,
AMERICAN SYNDICATED COLUMNIST,
ON THE ANNUAL TIME ADJUSTMENT

At Least There's Free Parking

The following classified ad appeared in a 1989 issue of the *Texas Bar Journal*:

"Small, highly disorganized . . . law firm, having characteristically waited past the last minute, frantically seeks associate with two to four years of experience in general business representation and business litigation. Successful applicant must be able to function with little or no guidance in extremely chaotic environment, and be able to stand long periods of indecision punctuated by short bursts of frantic activity. . . . Toleration of tobacco smoke required. Affinity for hard liquor recommended. . . . Free parking. . . . Only the stouthearted need apply."

J U D G E S

The judge weighs the arguments and puts a brave face
on the matter, and, since there must be a decision,
decides as he can, and hopes he has done justice.

RALPH WALDO EMERSON,
19TH-CENTURY AMERICAN WRITER AND POET

A judge is one more learned than witty,
more reverend than plausible, and more advised
than confident. Above all things, integrity is
their portion and proper virtue.

FRANCIS BACON,
16TH-CENTURY ENGLISH PHILOSOPHER AND WRITER

Appellate Division judges [are] the whores
who became madams.

MARTIN ERDMANN,
AMERICAN LAWYER

The right to one's day in court is meaningless if
the judge who hears the case lacks the talent,
experience and temperament that will enable him
to protect imperiled rights and to render a fair decision.

WILLIAM H. REHNQUIST,
SUPREME COURT JUSTICE

Judges are, in many respects, like parents. You have to
give them a good enough reason to do what you want.

DARLENE RICKER,
AMERICAN LAWYER AND LEGAL JOURNALIST

When did a judge ever think? He's paid not to.

MAXWELL ANDERSON, AMERICAN PLAYWRIGHT,
AND HAROLD HICKERSON, AMERICAN WRITER

It has been said that a judge is a member of the Bar
who once knew a governor.

CURTIS BOK,
PENNSYLVANIA SUPREME COURT JUSTICE

Judges are the weakest link in our system of justice,
and they are also the most protected.

ALAN DERSHOWITZ,
LAWYER AND HARVARD LAW PROFESSOR

For Heaven's sake discard the monstrous wig
which makes the English judges look like rats
peeping through bunches of oakum.

THOMAS JEFFERSON,
3RD PRESIDENT OF THE UNITED STATES

71

The ability of a judge to put himself into the shoes
of the men and women who appear before him
is the heart of being a decent judge.

JOSEPH A. WAPNER,
JUDGE OF THE TELEVISION SHOW THE PEOPLE'S COURT

Courtrooms contain every symbol of authority that
a set designer could imagine. Everyone stands up when
you come in. You wear a costume identifying you as,
if not quite divine, someone special.

IRVING R. KAUFMAN,
U.S. COURT OF APPEALS JUDGE

A judge is unjust who hears but one side of a case,
even though he decides it justly.

SENECA,
1ST-CENTURY B.C. ROMAN STATESMAN
AND PHILOSOPHER

72

I'll have you understand I am running this court,
and the law hasn't got a damn thing to do with it!

SAMUEL ERVIN, UNITED STATES SENATOR,
RECALLING AN OLD MAGISTRATE'S
WORDS TO A YOUNG ATTORNEY

There are no more reactionary people
in the world than judges.

**NIKOLAI LENIN,
RUSSIAN REVOLUTIONARY LEADER**

There should be many judges, for few will
always do the will of few.

**NICCOLO MACHIAVELLI,
15TH-CENTURY ITALIAN STATESMAN AND
POLITICAL PHILOSOPHER**

Judge: A law student who marks his own
examination papers.

**H. L. MENCKEN,
AMERICAN JOURNALIST**

The thing to fear is not the law but the judge.

RUSSIAN SAYING

The judge is condemned when the guilty is acquitted.

**PUBLILIUS SYRUS,
1ST-CENTURY B.C. ROMAN WRITER**

The acme of judicial distinction means the ability
to look a lawyer straight in the eyes for two hours and
not hear a damned word he says.

**JOHN MARSHALL,
SUPREME COURT JUSTICE**

74

The halls of justice. That's the only place you
see the justice, is in the halls.

**LENNY BRUCE,
AMERICAN COMEDIAN**

Judging is a lonely job in which a man is,
as near as may be, an island entire.

**ABE FORTAS,
SUPREME COURT JUSTICE**

I don't want to know what the law is,
I want to know who the judge is.

ROY M. COHN,
AMERICAN LAWYER

Judges are best in the beginning;
they deteriorate as time passes.

TACITUS,
1ST-CENTURY ROMAN HISTORIAN

A judge is merely a lawyer who has been benched.

CHARLES E. CLARK,
U.S. COURT OF APPEALS JUDGE

Knowing that religion does not furnish
grosser bigots than law,
I expect little from old judges.

THOMAS JEFFERSON,
3RD PRESIDENT OF THE UNITED STATES

The law is relaxed when the judge shows pity.

PUBLILIUS SYRUS,
1ST-CENTURY B.C. ROMAN WRITER

A good and faithful judge prefers what is right
to what is expedient.

HORACE,
1ST-CENTURY B.C. ROMAN POET AND SATIRIST

He who has the judge for his father goes into
court with an easy mind.

MIGUEL DE CERVANTES,
16TH-CENTURY SPANISH WRITER

The duty of a judge is to render justice;
his art is to delay it.

JEAN DE LA BRUYÈRE,
17TH-CENTURY FRENCH WRITER AND MORALIST

The judge is nothing but the law speaking.

BENJAMIN WHICHCOTE,
17TH-CENTURY ENGLISH PHILOSOPHICAL THEOLOGIAN

Judges are apt to be naive, simple-minded men.

OLIVER WENDELL HOLMES JR.,
SUPREME COURT JUSTICE

I will tell you about judges. You can take the most
mild-mannered and tender-hearted man you ever saw,
make him a judge for life, and his disposition to
tyrannize over people will grow with what he feeds on.

CHAMP CLARK,
UNITED STATES CONGRESSMAN

A lifetime diet of the law alone turns judges
into dull, dry husks.

WILLIAM O. DOUGLAS,
SUPREME COURT JUSTICE

A judge should be about sixty, clean shaven, with white
hair, china-blue eyes, and suffer from hemorrhoids
so that he will have that concerned look.

ANONYMOUS

Go Ahead. . . . Make My Day

When two attorneys vehemently argued over a
motion in her courtroom in 1992, Providence
(Rhode Island) Superior Court Judge Patricia Hurst
threatened to shoot them both—with a water pistol.

"I told them I have a good way of dealing with pro-
longed motions," the squirt-gun-toting judge told
reporters later.

Because she was seen brandishing the squirt gun in
court, Hurst was suspended for a month. Said Hurst, who
surrendered the water gun to her attorney, "I'm probably
guilty of having a bad sense of humor."

A Time To Rhyme

Michigan Appellate Court Judge John H. Gillis was so inspired by Joyce Kilmer's classic poem "Trees," that he wrote this verse in a 1983 opinion:

We thought that we would never see
A suit to compensate a tree.
A suit whose claim in tort is prest
Upon a mangled tree's behest;
A tree whose battered trunk was prest
Against a Chevy's crumpled crest;
A tree that faces each new day
With bark and limb in disarray;
A tree that may forever bear
A lasting need for tender care.
Flora lovers though we three,
We must uphold the court's decree.
Affirmed.

79

A Fine(d) Judge

An Alaskan judge levied a $500 fine on someone he knew better than anyone else—himself!

In 1991, Magistrate Craig McMahon of Bethel was swamped with 150 more cases than he had the previous year. To make matters worse, he had no secretary or computer. He had to write his decisions on an old typewriter.

Cases piled up and a few got lost on his desk. As a result, two alcohol prosecution cases had to be dismissed because McMahon had not scheduled speedy trials. "I felt pretty bad about losing the cases because of my procrastination," said the magistrate. "So I fined myself."

Short and Sweet

In 1990, Buffalo attorney Leonard Brizdle was arguing a case before New York Supreme Court Judge Carlton Fisher who called for briefs in ten days.

"Judge," said Brizdle, "if you can give me more time, I can write a shorter brief."

Declared Judge Fisher, "Briefs in twenty days!"

And Pick Up Your Socks
While You're At It

San Francisco Superior Court Judge Lucy Kelly McCabe often answers her own phone when it rings in chambers. Sometimes she wishes she hadn't.

That's because she occasionally receives an earful from chauvinist lawyers who verbally abuse her on the assumption that she is a lowly law clerk.

One day in 1992, Judge McCabe answered her phone and was given a tongue-lashing from an attorney who thought he was talking to her law clerk. He had just found out his case was taken off the calendar because a declaration wasn't signed. "Why didn't you call me?" he demanded.

"Because we're not your mother," snapped Judge McCabe before hanging up.

Bathroom Humor

When Maine Superior Court Justice Francis C. Marsano stepped into the bathroom off his chambers one memorable day in 1993, he heard an unusual click as the door closed behind him. The pin attached to the door handle that moves the bolt had broken.

No courthouse workers discovered Marsano before leaving for the day. Because the bathroom was windowless and concrete-walled, the judge was forced to spend the night there, sleeping on rolls of toilet paper.

After a clerk discovered Marsano's plight the next morning, workers used a sledgehammer to free the judge.

How did he view being locked in a courthouse bathroom for 16 hours? Said Marsano, "It puts a whole different spin on 'judicial seclusion.'"

J U R I E S

Percy Foreman and I once had an argument as to which of us
had picked the most stupid jury. I think I won with one that
returned a verdict which amounted to "Not guilty with a
recommendation of clemency because of reasonable doubt."

F. LEE BAILEY,
AMERICAN LAWYER

83

In the McFarland case the defendant set up the plea
of insanity, and succeeded in proving himself a fool.
And he was acquitted by a jury of his peers.

AMBROSE BIERCE,
AMERICAN WRITER

If the district attorney wanted, a grand jury
would indict a ham sandwich.

SYDNEY BIDDLE BARROWS,
"THE MAYFLOWER MADAM"

Today, the grand jury is the total captive of the prosecutor who, if he is candid, will concede that he can indict anybody, at any time, for almost anything, before any grand jury.

WILLIAM J. CAMPBELL,
U.S. DISTRICT COURT JUDGE

Juries . . . have the effect . . . of placing the control of the law in the hands of those who would be most apt to abuse it.

JAMES FENIMORE COOPER,
18TH-CENTURY AMERICAN WRITER

With attractive women [defendants] . . . juries sometimes have to be restrained from handing them a medal for their crimes.

JOHN MCGEORGE,
AUSTRALIAN PSYCHIATRIST

I never saw twelve men in my life, that,
if you could get them to understand a human case,
were not true and right.

CLARENCE DARROW,
AMERICAN LAWYER AND WRITER

A jury consists of twelve persons chosen to
decide who has the better lawyer.

ROBERT FROST,
AMERICAN POET

The average juror . . . wraps himself in civic
virtue. He's a judge now. He tries to act
the part and do the right thing.

JACOB D. FUCHSBERG,
PRESIDENT, AMERICAN TRIAL LAWYERS ASSOCIATION

Jury duty [is] a bog of quicksand on the path to justice.

SIDNEY BERNARD

Jury: Twelve men of limited information
and intelligence, chosen precisely because of their
lack of intellectual resilience.

**H. L. MENCKEN,
AMERICAN JOURNALIST**

We have a criminal jury system which is superior
to any in the world; and its efficiency is only marred by
the difficulty of finding twelve men every day who
don't know anything and can't read.

**MARK TWAIN,
AMERICAN WRITER AND HUMORIST**

In today's world a peer is not a hermit.

**NEWTON MINOW, FCC CHAIRMAN AND LAWYER,
ABOUT THE JUSTICE SYSTEM'S PRACTICE OF
EXCLUDING POTENTIAL JURORS
WHO FOLLOW THE NEWS**

I would rather have my fate in the hands of 23 representative citizens of the county than in the hands of a politically appointed judge.

ROBERT MORGENTHAU,
NEW YORK CITY DISTRICT ATTORNEY,
DEFENDING THE SECRECY
OF GRAND JURY PROCEEDINGS

The jury is, above all, a political institution, and it must be regarded in this light in order to be duly appreciated.

ALEXIS DE TOCQUEVILLE,
19TH-CENTURY FRENCH STATESMAN AND WRITER

87

We, the jury, find our client not guilty.

VERDICT OF A JURY IN THE MUNICIPAL
COURT AT FORT SMITH, ARKANSAS,
IN A DRUNKENNESS CASE, DEC. 2, 1933

I have what jurors want. They want charisma.
They want a fight in the courtroom.
They don't want placidity. They don't want
a one-dimensional lawsuit. They came here for a show.
And they want to do what's right.

PHILIP CORBOY,
AMERICAN LAWYER

The jury is a collection of sedentary owls.

ELBERT HUBBARD,
AMERICAN WRITER AND EDITOR

A jury is a group of twelve people of average ignorance.

HERBERT SPENCER,
19TH-CENTURY ENGLISH PHILOSOPHER

It is the "ordinariness" of the jury that finally
emerges as its unique strength.

MELVYN B. ZERMAN,
AMERICAN WRITER

Jury Prudence

Attorney Richard Glasson of Carson City, Nevada, was defending a 1989 slip-and-fall case in Douglas County District Court where the plaintiff's attorney was being especially annoying.

Just before the lunch recess, the jury sent out a note to the court which read: "We, the jury, in the interest of an expeditious trial, and for the general reduction of immaterial and repetitious questioning, do hereby recommend that a shocking collar device be securely fastened to plaintiff's counsel. The control of said device shall be entrusted to a responsible member of the jury panel to be selected following the next recess. We thank you for your support."

Plaintiff's counsel went out in the hall with Glasson and immediately settled the case.

I'll Sleep on It

Judge Gerald Kalina of Hastings, Minnesota, was asking prospective jurors at the outset of a 1990 trial whether any of them had scheduling conflicts or illnesses that might prevent their serving that day.

One candidate raised his hand and said, "I suffer from narcolepsy and I'm worried that if I am chosen, I might nod off or fall asleep during part of the trial."

"Well, we can't have that," replied Kalina. "That's the job of the judge!"

W I T N E S S E S

For a plot hatched in hell, don't expect angels for witnesses.

ROBERT PERRY,
AMERICAN LAWYER

In response to the question: "Is that
your conclusion that this man is a malingerer?"
Dr. Unsworth responded: "I wouldn't be testifying
if I didn't think so, unless I was on the other side,
then it would be a post traumatic condition."

LADNER V. HIGGINS,
1954 LOUISIANA APPELLATE COURT

91

I think that one of the most fundamental
responsibilities . . . is to give testimony in a court
of law, to give it honestly and willingly.

ADLAI E. STEVENSON,
AMERICAN LAWYER AND DIPLOMAT

Lies and liars come in all types of packages.
At some point the difference between an
honest witness and a dishonest one is attitude.
Honest witnesses remember the facts the
way they must have been, dishonest
witnesses remember them
the way they should have been.

**ERIC ZAGRANS,
AMERICAN LAWYER**

Sleepy Heads

Phoenix lawyer Clint Batterton was trying to lighten his cross-examination of an anesthesiologist who was a plaintiff in a securities fraud case in 1988.

"I guess that means you and I are in the same business because we both put people to sleep," Batterton joked.

"Yes," replied the witness. "But I wake them up."

THE SUPREME COURT

Who is to say that five men 10 years ago
were right whereas five men looking the other
direction today are wrong.

**HARRY A. BLACKMUN, SUPREME COURT JUSTICE,
ON PRIOR COURT DECISIONS,
ESPECIALLY 5-4 VOTES**

93

Something about our courtroom scares lawyers
to death. Some fellows have fainted.

**WILLIAM J. BRENNAN JR.,
SUPREME COURT JUSTICE**

If you took the brains of the majority of the Supreme
Court and put them into the head of a bird, the bird
would fly backward for ever and ever and ever.

**BENJAMIN HOOKS,
CHAIRMAN, NAACP**

They were political animals before
they got to the Supreme Court,
and they don't change when they get there.

**CHRISTINE KELLETT, LAW PROFESSOR, DICKINSON SCHOOL,
COMMENTING THAT SUPREME COURT JUSTICES ARE
IN STEP WITH THE POPULACE ON MOST ISSUES**

You know, it's almost time to turn back the clock.
That's right, the Supreme Court's back in session.

**JAY LENO,
AMERICAN COMEDIAN**

The people can change Congress but only God can
change the Supreme Court.

**GEORGE W. NORRIS,
UNITED STATES SENATOR**

For the most part . . . we function as nine small
independent law firms.

**LEWIS F. POWELL JR.,
SUPREME COURT JUSTICE**

We're all eccentrics. We're nine prima donnas.

HARRY A. BLACKMUN,
SUPREME COURT JUSTICE

We current justices read the Constitution in the only
way that we can—as 20th-century Americans.

WILLIAM J. BRENNAN JR.,
SUPREME COURT JUSTICE

If this country wanted its Supreme Court to reflect
the immediate social or political wishes of the nation's
people, it would provide for the election of the court.
And if the founding fathers had wanted it that way,
they could have said so—or at least hinted at it.
They did just the opposite. They designed a system
that tried to immunize the court from the changing
moods and passions of the people.

MARIO CUOMO,
AMERICAN POLITICIAN

95

Our Constitution was not written in the sands to
be washed away by each wave of new judges blown in
by each successive political wind.

**HUGO L. BLACK,
SUPREME COURT JUSTICE**

In an era of "sound bites" and instant opinion
polls it is dangerous to apply broad labels
to a single [Supreme Court] term.

**LEWIS F. POWELL JR.,
SUPREME COURT JUSTICE**

One puts on black robes to scare the hell
out of white people, while the other puts on white robes
to scare the hell out of blacks.

**MORRIS K. UDALL, UNITED STATES CONGRESSMAN,
CONTRASTING SUPREME COURT JUSTICES AND
KU KLUX KLAN MEMBERS**

Whenever you put a man on the Supreme Court
he ceases to be your friend.

HARRY S TRUMAN,
33RD PRESIDENT OF THE UNITED STATES

Books? Who Needs Books?

When the Supreme Court was moved from the old capital of Philadelphia to Washington, D.C. in 1800, the government failed to provide the justices with law books.

Said Robert H. Jackson, author of *The Supreme Court in the American System of Government*, "[That] accounts for the high quality of early opinions."

97

CODES OF CONDUCT

Lawyers know that no other group or profession
sets higher ethical standards, disciplines itself
so rigorously, [and] contributes so much
unpaid service to the public.

DAVID R. BRINK, PRESIDENT,
AMERICAN BAR ASSOCIATION

Nobody has a more sacred obligation to obey the law
than those who make the law.

SOPHOCLES,
5TH-CENTURY B.C. GREEK DRAMATIST

I didn't really mean that all lawyers are dishonest.
Just that the honest ones are all poor.

ANN GERBER,
AMERICAN JOURNALIST

An eminent lawyer cannot be a dishonest man.
Tell me a man is dishonest, and I will answer he is no
lawyer. He cannot be, because he is careless and
reckless of justice; the law is not in his heart [and] . . .
is not the standard and rule of his conduct.

DANIEL WEBSTER,
18TH-CENTURY AMERICAN STATESMAN,
ORATOR, AND LAWYER

If young people entering the law are honest with
themselves, have the ability to say no, resolve
not to serve themselves more than their clients, and
commit themselves to the oath of the court,
we'll all be the better for it.

PAMELA ANN RYMER,
LOS ANGELES FEDERAL JUDGE

I'm not an ambulance chaser. I'm usually there
before the ambulance.

MELVIN BELLI,
AMERICAN LAWYER

The excesses of today's legal system and those who profess to be its servants in fact amount to a serious problem and are at the root of a festering public disrespect for the law.

SAMUEL JAN BRAKEL,
AMERICAN LAWYER

In civilized life, law floats in a sea of ethics. Each is indispensable to civilization. Without law, we should be at the mercy of the least scrupulous; without ethics, law could not exist.

EARL WARREN,
SUPREME COURT JUSTICE

103

Too many lawyers have forgotten that the main purpose of the law profession is to serve the public interest.

PETER BROWN,
AMERICAN LAWYER

You just had to take the practical view that a man
always lied on his own behalf, and paid his lawyer,
who was an expert, a professional liar,
to show him new and better ways of lying.

**JAMES GOULD COZZENS,
AMERICAN WRITER**

I don't see why we should not come out roundly
and say that one of the functions of a lawyer
is to lie for his client; and on rare occasions,
as I think I have shown, I believe it is.

**CHARLES P. CURTIS,
AMERICAN LAWYER**

Bar associations are notoriously reluctant to disbar
or even suspend a member unless he has murdered
a judge downtown at high noon, in the presence
of the entire Committee on Ethical Practices.

**SYDNEY J. HARRIS,
BRITISH-AMERICAN WRITER**

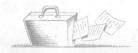

No poet ever interpreted nature as freely
as a lawyer interprets truth.

**JEAN GIRAUDOUX,
19TH-CENTURY FRENCH PLAYWRIGHT**

What do you get in place of a conscience?
Don't answer, I know: a lawyer.

**KIRK DOUGLAS AS DETECTIVE JIM MCLEOD,
IN THE FILM DETECTIVE STORY**

The ethical distinction between lying to a jury
and pulling the wool over its eyes is surely a fine one.

**PHILLIP E. JOHNSON,
LAW PROFESSOR, UNIVERSITY OF CALIFORNIA**

It is difficult to overestimate how responsible
Watergate was for putting the spotlight on legal ethics.

**MICHAEL ALAN SCHWARTZ,
AMERICAN JOURNALIST**

Just addressed the California State Legislature and helped them pass a bill to form a lawyers' association to regulate their conduct. Personally I don't think you can make a lawyer honest by an act of the Legislature. You've got to work on his conscience. And his lack of conscience is what makes him a lawyer.

**WILL ROGERS,
AMERICAN ACTOR AND HUMORIST**

Professional Discourtesy

George Ade, a well-known humorist in the early part of the century, had just finished a delightful speech at a banquet and sat down to applause from the crowd.

The master of ceremonies, a well-known lawyer, got to his feet, shoved his hands into his pants pockets, as was his habit, and asked the crowd, "Doesn't it strike anyone as a little unusual that a professional humorist should be funny?"

When the laughter from the audience subsided, Ade stood up and told the crowd, "Doesn't it strike anyone as a little unusual that a lawyer should have his hands in his own pockets?"

"Nod" Guilty

Judge James Darrah of the San Joaquin County (California) Superior Court granted a convicted murderer a new trial in 1989—because the judge confessed that he had fallen asleep during part of a defense witness's testimony.

Judge Darrah found Tab Lee Bennett guilty of murder. But then the judge reconsidered and filed his own affidavit, swearing he had been asleep for 13 minutes of testimony that focused on the description of the scene of the crime. The judge said he couldn't be sure that nodding off didn't have some affect on the verdict.

GOVERNMENT

The more perfect civilization is, the less occasion
it has for government, because the more it does to
regulate its own affairs, and govern itself. . . .
All the great laws of society are laws of nature.

**THOMAS PAINE,
18TH-CENTURY BRITISH-BORN AMERICAN
POLITICAL PHILOSOPHER AND WRITER**

I believe that the law was made for man
and not man for the law; that government is the
servant of the people and not their master.

**JOHN D. ROCKEFELLER JR.,
AMERICAN OIL MAGNATE AND PHILANTHROPIST**

The execution of the laws is more important
than the making of them.

**THOMAS JEFFERSON,
3RD PRESIDENT OF THE UNITED STATES**

The last bastion of protecting everyone's
right to freedom is a court of law.

**RICHARD ISRAELS,
CANADIAN LAWYER**

Can any of you seriously say the Bill of Rights
could get through Congress today? It wouldn't
even get out of committee.

**F. LEE BAILEY,
AMERICAN LAWYER**

Law is not self-executing. Unfortunately, at times its
execution rests in the hands of those who are faithless
to it. And even when its enforcement is committed to
those who revere it, law merely deters some human beings
from offending, and punishes other human beings for
offending. It does not make men good. This task can
be performed only by ethics or religion or morality.

**SAMUEL ERVIN JR.,
UNITED STATES SENATOR**

From Antigone through Martin Luther to Martin
Luther King Jr., the issue of liberty has turned on the
existence of a higher law than that of the State.

**MILTON MAYER,
AMERICAN JOURNALIST**

Good laws, if they are not obeyed, do not
constitute good government.

**ARISTOTLE,
4TH-CENTURY B.C. GREEK PHILOSOPHER**

A government of laws, and not of men.

**JOHN ADAMS,
2ND PRESIDENT OF THE UNITED STATES**

All associations are dangerous to good Government . . .
and associations of Lawyers the most dangerous
of any next to the Military.

**CADWALLADER COLDEN,
17TH-CENTURY IRISH-BORN AMERICAN POLITICIAN**

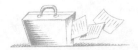

Open Season on Lawyers

Before adjourning its session in 1989, the Virginia legislature jokingly considered a bill establishing a new sport—hunting for attorneys!

The bill was referred to the state game board for a determination of whether lawyers should be deemed a nuisance species. Under the bill, using cash as bait and shouting "whiplash" and "ambulance" to trap lawyers would be strictly prohibited.

The bill for an open season on lawyers failed to pass.

LAW SCHOOL

Doctors and lawyers must go to school for years
and years, often with little sleep and with
great sacrifice to their first wives.

**ROY BLOUNT JR.,
AMERICAN WRITER**

Be prepared, be sharp, be careful, and use the King's
English well. And you can forget all the [other rules]
unless you remember one more: Get paid.

**ROBERT N. C. NIX, UNITED STATES CONGRESSMAN,
GIVING ADVICE TO YOUNG LAWYERS AT HIS SON'S
GRADUATION FROM LAW SCHOOL**

Law school taught me one thing:
how to take two situations that are exactly the same
and show how they are different.

**HART POMERANTZ,
AMERICAN LAWYER**

Law students are trained in the case method,
and, to the lawyer, everything in life looks like a case.
His first thought in the morning is how
to handle the case of the ringing alarm clock.

EDWARD B. PACKARD JR.,
AMERICAN LAWYER

We must begin to train lawyers the minute they
walk into law school to tell the truth. They must
immediately begin to learn the business of representing
people. They must be assigned cases the first day.

GERRY SPENCE,
AMERICAN LAWYER

Law school has been described as a place for the
accumulation of learning. First-year students bring
some in; third-year students take none away.
Hence it accumulates.

DANIEL R. WHITE,
AMERICAN WRITER

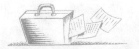

Good law schools teach you to think
like lawyers. But the top law schools teach
young people to think; just to think.
And that makes a potentially great lawyer.

**NORM SHERMAN,
AMERICAN LAWYER**

Leave it to Beaver

As a young deputy district attorney in Kern County, California, in 1973, H. Dennis Beaver was trying a consumer fraud case before Judge Walter Conley. But the judge rapidly grew exasperated with the rookie lawyer's line of questioning.

"If you keep on asking these idiotic questions, I am going to send you some place where you have never been," the judge warned Beaver.

"You mean jail, your honor?" Beaver asked.

"No," replied the judge. "Law school!"

And What About the Benefits?

When Judge Richard Neely of Charleston, West Virginia, was seeking new law clerks in 1991, he ran the following ad in the *University of Virginia Law Weekly*:

"West Virginia's infamous once and future Justice Richard Neely, America's laziest and dumbest judge, seeks a bright person to keep him from looking stupid. Preference will be given to U. Va. law students who studied interesting but useless subjects at snobby schools. If you are dead drunk and miss the interviews, send letters."

115

O B E Y I N G   T H E   L A W

The mass of the people have nothing to do
with the laws but to obey them.

**SAMUEL HORSLEY,
18TH-CENTURY ENGLISH BISHOP**

One has not only a legal but a moral responsibility
to obey just laws. Conversely, one has a moral
responsibility to disobey unjust laws.

**DR. MARTIN LUTHER KING JR.,
AMERICAN CLERGYMAN AND CIVIL RIGHTS LEADER**

No man in this country is so high that he is above
the law. No officer of the law may set that law
at defiance with impunity. All the officers of the
government, from the highest to the lowest,
are creatures of the law, and are bound to obey it.

**SAMUEL F. MILLER,
19TH-CENTURY AMERICAN JUDGE**

In a democracy only those laws which have their bases
in folkways or the approval of strong groups have a
chance of being enforced.

**ABRAHAM MYERSON,
RUSSIAN-AMERICAN NEUROPSYCHIATRIST**

There's a lot of law at the end of a nightstick.

**GROVER A. WHALEN,
NEW YORK CITY POLICE COMMISSIONER**

Anyone who takes it upon himself, on his private
authority, to break a bad law, thereby authorizes
everyone else to break the good ones.

**DENIS DIDEROT,
18TH-CENTURY FRENCH ENCYCLOPEDIST**

Good men must not obey the laws too well.

**RALPH WALDO EMERSON,
19TH-CENTURY AMERICAN POET AND WRITER**

Laws were made to be broken.

**CHRISTOPHER NORTH,
18TH-CENTURY SCOTTISH WRITER**

The best use of good laws is to teach men to trample
bad laws under their feet.

**WENDELL PHILLIPS,
19TH-CENTURY AMERICAN ORATOR AND REFORMER**

There are not enough jails, not enough policemen,
not enough courts to enforce a law not
supported by the people.

**HUBERT HUMPHREY,
38TH VICE PRESIDENT OF THE UNITED STATES**

To make laws that man cannot, and will not obey,
serves to bring all law into contempt.

**ELIZABETH CADY STANTON,
19TH-CENTURY AMERICAN SUFFRAGIST**

There is no man so good, who, were he to submit all his thoughts and action to the laws, would not deserve hanging ten times in his life.

MICHEL DE MONTAIGNE,
16TH-CENTURY FRENCH WRITER

It ain't no sin if you crack a few laws now and then, just so long as you don't break any.

MAE WEST AS PEACHES O'DAY,
IN THE FILM EVERY DAY'S A HOLIDAY

Late every night in Connecticut, lights go out in the cities and towns, and citizens by tens of thousands proceed zestfully to break the law. Of course, there is always a witness to the crime—but as though to make the law completely unenforceable, Connecticut forbids spouses from testifying against one another.

TIME,
ON THE CONNECTICUT LAW AGAINST
CONTRACEPTIVES, 1961

No man is above the law and no man is below it;
nor do we ask any man's permission
when we ask him to obey it.

**THEODORE ROOSEVELT,
26TH PRESIDENT OF THE UNITED STATES**

The notorious lawlessness of the Commander has
passed into a proverb, familiar to man-of-war's men:
The law was not made for the Captain!

**HERMAN MELVILLE,
19TH-CENTURY AMERICAN WRITER**

Whether ours shall continue to be a government of
laws and not of men is now for Congress and
ultimately the American people to decide.

**ARCHIBALD COX, WATERGATE PROSECUTOR,
AFTER BEING DISMISSED BY PRESIDENT RICHARD NIXON
BECAUSE HE REFUSED TO DROP HIS LAWSUIT
TO OBTAIN WATERGATE-RELATED
WHITE HOUSE TAPES**

When the President does it, that means it is not illegal.

**RICHARD NIXON,
37TH PRESIDENT OF THE UNITED STATES**

If Nixon is not forced to turn over tapes of his
conversations with the ring of men who were
conversing on their violations of the law,
then liberty will soon be dead in this nation.

**WILLIAM O. DOUGLAS,
SUPREME COURT JUSTICE**

121

The illegal we do immediately.
The unconstitutional takes a little longer.

**HENRY KISSINGER, NATIONAL SECURITY ADVISOR
AND SECRETARY OF STATE IN THE NIXON ADMINISTRATION**

A man's respect for law and order exists in precise
relationship to the size of his paycheck.

**ADAM CLAYTON POWELL JR.,
AMERICAN CLERGYMAN AND UNITED STATES CONGRESSMAN**

Laws made by common consent must not
be trampled on by individuals.

GEORGE WASHINGTON,
1ST PRESIDENT OF THE UNITED STATES

Winner Take All

Attorney Arlo Sommervold of Sioux Falls, South Dakota, was representing a defendant charged with stealing hogs during a 1991 trial.

After Sommervold put on a spirited defense, the jury deliberated for a short while and then returned with its verdict. The jury foreman announced, "We the jury acquit the defendant."

Sommervold turned to shake hands with his client, who then asked, "Does this mean I can keep the hogs?"

J U S T I C E

Wrong must not win by technicalities.

AESCHYLUS,
6TH-CENTURY B.C. GREEK DRAMATIST

When it comes to justice, I take no prisoners
and I don't believe in compromising.

MARY FRANCES BERRY,
AMERICAN LEGAL SCHOLAR AND
CIVIL RIGHTS ACTIVIST

123

But let judgment run down as waters,
and righteousness as a mighty stream.

AMOS, 5:24

Get out of the way of Justice. She is blind.

STANISLAW LEC,
CZECH WRITER

Though justice moves slowly, it seldom fails
to overtake the wicked.

HORACE,
1ST-CENTURY B.C. ROMAN POET AND SATIRIST

The wheels of justice . . . they're square wheels.

BARBARA CORCORAN,
AMERICAN WRITER

There is no such thing as justice—in or out of court.

CLARENCE DARROW,
AMERICAN LAWYER AND WRITER

Justice is the end of government.

DANIEL DEFOE,
17TH-CENTURY ENGLISH WRITER

Sir, I say that justice is truth in action.

BENJAMIN DISRAELI,
19TH-CENTURY BRITISH PRIME MINISTER

124

I tell ye Hogan's right when he says: "Justice is blind."
Blind she is, an' deaf an' dumb an' has a wooden leg!

MR. DOOLEY [FINLEY PETER DUNNE],
AMERICAN HUMORIST

If we are to keep our democracy, there must be one
commandment: Thou shalt not ration justice.

LEARNED HAND,
U.S. COURT OF APPEALS JUDGE

Justice, n. A commodity which in a more or less
adulterated condition the State sells to the citizen as a
reward for his allegiance, taxes, and personal service.

AMBROSE BIERCE,
AMERICAN WRITER

The primary duty of a lawyer engaged in
public prosecution is not to convict, but to see
that justice is done.

CANONS OF PROFESSIONAL ETHICS,
CANON 5

Justice is incidental to law and order.

J. EDGAR HOOVER,
DIRECTOR, FBI

Justice should remove the bandage from her eyes
long enough to distinguish between
the vicious and the unfortunate.

ROBERT G. INGERSOLL,
19TH-CENTURY AMERICAN LAWYER

Justice is the right of the weaker.

JOSEPH JOUBERT,
18TH-CENTURY FRENCH WRITER AND MORALIST

As soon as I set myself up as the judge and jury,
I might as well be the executioner.

RICHARD ISRAELS,
CANADIAN LAWYER

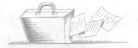

White folks don't want peace; they want quiet.
The price you pay for peace is justice. Until there
is justice, there will be no peace and quiet.

JESSE JACKSON,
AMERICAN CLERGYMAN AND
CIVIL RIGHTS LEADER

A right is not what someone gives you; it's what
no one can take from you.

RAMSEY CLARK,
U.S. ATTORNEY GENERAL

127

Justice delayed is democracy denied.

ROBERT F. KENNEDY,
U.S. ATTORNEY GENERAL

I have a saying—there's no justice in the law.

ELLEN MORPHONIOS,
AMERICAN JUDGE ALSO KNOWN AS
"MAXIMUM MORPHONIOS"

This court will not deny the equal protection
of the law to the unwashed, unshod,
unkempt, and uninhibited.

**HERMAN WEINKRANTZ,
AMERICAN JUDGE**

There is no authority without justice.

**NAPOLEON I,
EMPEROR OF FRANCE**

Justice and judgment lie often a world apart.

**EMMELINE PANKHURST,
ENGLISH SUFFRAGIST**

The fundamentals of justice are that
no one shall suffer wrong, and that the
public good be served.

**CICERO,
2ND-CENTURY B.C. ROMAN STATESMAN,
ORATOR, AND WRITER**

Fairness is what justice really is.

POTTER STEWART,
SUPREME COURT JUSTICE

Judging from the main portions of
the history of the world so far,
justice is always in jeopardy.

WALT WHITMAN,
19TH-CENTURY AMERICAN POET

Unless justice be done to others
it will not be done to us.

WOODROW WILSON,
28TH PRESIDENT OF THE UNITED STATES

Justice, though she's painted blind
Is to the weaker side inclined.

SAMUEL BUTLER,
17TH-CENTURY ENGLISH SATIRICAL POET

Justice is like a train that's nearly always late.

YEVGENY YEVTUSHENKO,
RUSSIAN POET

The achievement of justice is an endless process.

JOHN F. KENNEDY,
35TH PRESIDENT OF THE UNITED STATES

Justice is lame as well as blind.

THOMAS OTWAY,
17TH-CENTURY ENGLISH DRAMATIST

Rather suffer an injustice than commit one.

YIDDISH PROVERB

Every virtue is included in the idea of justice,
and every just man is good.

THEOGNIS,
6TH-CENTURY B.C. GREEK POET

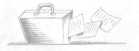

Let justice be done, though the world perish.

MOTTO OF FERDINAND I,
HOLY ROMAN EMPEROR

Justice may wink a while, but see at last.

THOMAS MIDDLETON,
16TH-CENTURY ENGLISH DRAMATIST

You may not find justice in the courtroom,
but you usually get what you deserve.

DAVID SPICER,
AMERICAN LAWYER

131

One hour of justice is worth a hundred of prayer.

ARAB PROVERB

Justice is always violent to the party offending,
for every man is innocent in his own eyes.

DANIEL DEFOE,
17TH-CENTURY ENGLISH WRITER

Justice is my being allowed to do whatever I like.
Injustice is whatever prevents my doing so.

SAMUEL BUTLER,
19TH-CENTURY ENGLISH JOURNALIST AND WRITER

Justice is the great standing policy of civil society.

EDMUND BURKE,
18TH-CENTURY ENGLISH STATESMAN AND ORATOR

Absolute freedom mocks at justice.
Absolute justice denies freedom.

ALBERT CAMUS,
FRENCH WRITER

Justice? You get justice in the next world,
in this world you have the law.

WILLIAM GADDIS,
WRITER

Whereas in Greek the idea of justice was akin to harmony, in Hebrew it is akin to holiness.

JOSEPH H. HERTZ,
BRITISH-BORN HUNGARIAN RABBI

Justice is the earnest and constant will to render to every man his due. The precepts of the law are these: to live honorably, to injure no other man, to render to every man his due.

JUSTINIAN I,
EMPEROR OF BYZANTINE

133

The love of justice is simply, in the majority of men, the fear of suffering injustice.

FRANÇOIS DE LA ROCHEFOUCAULD,
17TH-CENTURY FRENCH WRITER

Justice is the only thing that allowed the
human race to stop living as animals and to
start living as human beings.

**FRANK W. WILSON,
AMERICAN JUDGE**

It Takes Two

Judge William C. Miller of Montgomery County, Maryland, was hearing a 1990 case in which the defendant had skipped his court date.

Miller announced he was going to issue a bench warrant to have the defendant picked up.

"You can't do that," said the public defender. "The man is a schizophrenic."

"In that case," replied the judge, "I'll issue two."

Seeking Body and Soul

Lawyer Amy Jackson of the Legal Aid Society of Salt Lake City, Utah, was discussing a family law case with her paralegal one day in 1993. The client had filled out an application with the legal aid society that stated she wanted "soul" custody.

Seeing the error, the paralegal remarked, "I'm not sure we can get jurisdiction."

House Calls

Doctors may not make house calls anymore, but Memphis Criminal Court Judge Joe B. Brown has.

The former criminal defense attorney has on several occasions accepted guilty pleas from burglars and then attached an unusual condition. Their victims get to drop by the thieves' houses and take something from *them*!

In 1991, Brown's sentence was carried out by business executive Lionel Winston, whose housekeeper had

stolen from him. Accompanied by Judge Brown and a sheriff's deputy, Winston paid two unannounced visits to the ex-housekeeper's house and claimed two coats that he later gave away.

"I asked [the convict] how it felt to lose a possession and he said, 'Not so good,'" Winston recalled. "I said, 'Now you know how it felt.'"

A Wife Sentence

A judge known for his unusual sentences made marriage a mandatory condition in a defendant's plea bargain.

When Kevin Musser was convicted of assaulting his live-in girlfriend in 1992, Citrus County (Florida) Judge Gary Graham told him, "You have a choice. Marry the mother of your children and get a year's probation or never see her again and get a year in jail."

Musser chose to be sentenced to marriage rather than the hoosegow.

And Toto Too?

Referring to a scene from the classic movie *The Wizard of Oz* nearly got a defense attorney cited for contempt.

During sentencing in a criminal trial in Dayton (Ohio) Municipal Court in 1989, Judge Michael Merz read aloud from the defendant's rap sheet, "Convicted of manslaughter in 1957 in Kansas." Judge Merz then asked defense counsel George E. Zimmerman, "Do you have any suggestions as to how we can get your client back to Kansas?"

Replied the quick-witted attorney, "How about if I have him click his heels together three times?" Realizing his wit might get him into trouble, Zimmerman added, "Oh, I'm sorry, your honor."

"That's too funny to be contemptuous, counselor," said Judge Merz. "Perhaps the workhouse will better suit him for the next six months."

INJUSTICE

When one has been threatened
with a great injustice,
one accepts a smaller as a favor.

JANE WELSH CARLYLE,
19TH-CENTURY SCOTTISH POET

"No, no!" said the Queen.
"Sentence first—verdict afterwards."

FROM LEWIS CARROLL'S
ALICE'S ADVENTURES IN WONDERLAND

We have accumulated a wealth of historical
experience which confirms our belief that
the scales of American justice are out of balance.

ANGELA YVONNE DAVIS,
AMERICAN CIVIL RIGHTS ACTIVIST AND EDUCATOR

Extreme justice is extreme injustice.

CICERO,
1ST-CENTURY B.C. ROMAN STATESMAN,
ORATOR, AND WRITER

National injustice is the surest road
to national downfall.

WILLIAM EVARTS,
19TH-CENTURY AMERICAN LAWYER

Justice delayed is justice denied.

WILLIAM E. GLADSTONE,
19TH-CENTURY BRITISH STATESMAN

Since when do you have to agree with people
to defend them from injustice?

LILLIAN HELLMAN,
AMERICAN DRAMATIST

Injustice anywhere is a threat to justice everywhere.

DR. MARTIN LUTHER KING JR.,
AMERICAN CLERGYMAN AND CIVIL RIGHTS LEADER

Injustice is relatively easy to bear;
what stings is justice.

H. L. MENCKEN,
AMERICAN JOURNALIST

A kingdom founded on injustice never lasts.

SENECA,
1ST-CENTURY ROMAN STATESMAN
AND PHILOSOPHER

One had better die fighting against injustice
than die like a dog or a rat in a trap.

IDA B. WELLS,
AMERICAN JOURNALIST

It would have cost me more trouble to escape
from injustice, than it does to submit to it.

**JEANNE-MARIE ROLAND,
18TH-CENTURY FRENCH REVOLUTIONARY**

You've Got Him!

During a 1991 civil case in Cook County (Illinois) Circuit Court, an attorney was doing a particularly skillful job of cross-examining a witness.

Question by question, he laid a trap that seemed inescapable. When he asked the final question, the judge could stand it no longer. Before the witness could answer, the judge yelled, "You've got him! You've got him!"

The case settled during a short recess.

THE WHEELS OF JUSTICE

In the strange heat all litigation brings to bear
on things, the very process of litigation fosters the
most profound misunderstandings in the world.

RENATA ADLER,
ITALIAN-BORN AMERICAN WRITER,
FILM CRITIC, AND PHILOSOPHER

As a people we must somehow get over the notion
that the solution to every problem is a lawsuit.

ERNEST CONINE,
AMERICAN JOURNALIST

Criticizing lawyers for lawsuits is like criticizing
linebackers for knocking people down.

DALE DAUTEN,
NEWSPAPER COLUMNIST

More lawsuits may not be good for large corporations,
but they are good for justice and society, especially if
brought by the powerless against the powerful.

**ALAN DERSHOWITZ,
LAWYER AND HARVARD LAW PROFESSOR**

The courtrooms of America all too often
have Piper Cub advocates trying to handle
the controls of Boeing 747 litigation.

**WARREN BURGER,
SUPREME COURT JUSTICE**

To seek the redress of grievances by going to law
is like sheep running for shelter to a bramble bush.

**LEWIS W. DILLWYN,
18TH-CENTURY ENGLISH NATURALIST**

A lean compromise is better than a fat lawsuit.

ENGLISH PROVERB

A lawsuit is a fruit tree planted in a lawyer's garden.

ITALIAN PROVERB

The American liability lawsuit mess is the corporate version of the weather—everyone talks about it, but nothing ever happens.

THE CORPORATE BOARD

We lawyers know well, and may cite high authority for it if required, that life would be intolerable if every man insisted on his legal rights to the full.

**FREDERICK POLLOCK,
ENGLISH JUDGE**

147

Never stir up litigation. A worse man can scarcely be found than one who does this.

**ABRAHAM LINCOLN,
16TH PRESIDENT OF THE UNITED STATES**

It is becoming increasingly clear that litigation
is threatening our national economic viability.
Sheer numbers tell the story.

J. DANFORTH QUAYLE,
44TH VICE PRESIDENT OF THE UNITED STATES

A simple principle supports the medical litigation
industry. Sue often enough, and eventually a
sympathetic jury will return an outlandish verdict.

LINDA SEEBACH,
AMERICAN JOURNALIST

The issues can be analyzed in pages
less than fifty
If plaintiffs could with thought and words
endeavor to be thrifty.

ASHER RUBIN,
CALIFORNIA DEPUTY ATTORNEY GENERAL,
REPLYING IN RHYME TO THE LAWYERS
FOR THE OPPOSITION WHO SUBMITTED
THEIR SECOND REQUEST TO FILE A BRIEF THAT
EXCEEDED THE COURT'S 50-PAGE LIMIT

Litigation should be a last resort, not a knee-jerk reflex.

IRVING S. SHAPIRO,
AMERICAN INDUSTRIALIST

We have too many lawyers chasing too many dollars
through too many endless lawsuits,
and it is time to do something about it.

CASPAR W. WEINBERGER,
PUBLISHER OF FORBES

Litigation takes the place of sex at middle age.

GORE VIDAL,
AMERICAN WRITER

Four out of five potential litigants will settle their
disputes the first day they come together, if you will
put the idea of arbitration into their heads.

MOSES HENRY GROSSMAN,
AMERICAN JUDGE

That's Not What I Pictured

Pennsylvania lawyer James Sposito sued the publisher of a phone book in 1989 for defamation of character and breach of contract.

Sposito paid for an ad in the phone book promoting his specialty—personal injury cases. The ad was supposed to be illustrated with a picture of two vehicles crashing. Unfortunately, the vehicles pictured next to his name in the ad were ambulances.

THE TRIAL

Trial, n. A formal inquiry designed to prove and
put upon record the blameless characters
of judges, advocates and jurors.

AMBROSE BIERCE,
AMERICAN WRITER

The trial of a case (is) a three-legged stool—
a judge and two advocates.

WARREN BURGER,
SUPREME COURT JUSTICE

I love judges, and I love courts. They are my ideals,
that typify on earth what we shall meet hereafter
in heaven under a just God.

WILLIAM HOWARD TAFT,
27TH PRESIDENT OF THE UNITED STATES

The penalty for laughing in the courtroom
is six months in jail: if it were not for this penalty,
the jury would never hear the evidence.

**H. L. MENCKEN,
AMERICAN JOURNALIST**

This is a court of law, young man,
not a court of justice.

**OLIVER WENDELL HOLMES JR.,
SUPREME COURT JUSTICE**

This is not a court of love, of compassion,
but a court of law.

**DANIEL COBURN,
AMERICAN LAWYER**

All sides in a trial want to hide
at least some of the truth.

**ALAN DERSHOWITZ,
LAWYER AND HARVARD LAW PROFESSOR**

Laws are a dead letter without courts to expound
and define their true meaning and operation.

ALEXANDER HAMILTON,
AMERICAN STATESMAN

It's the greatest murder trial of the century—
about every two years another one of 'em comes along.

FRANCES NOYES HART,
AMERICAN WRITER

153

The criminal trial today is . . . a kind of show-jumping
contest in which the rider for the prosecution must
clear every obstacle to succeed.

ROBERT MARK,
BRITISH POLICE COMMISSIONER

Judge: Are you trying to show contempt for the court?
Flower Belle Lee: No, I'm doing my best to hide it.

W. C. FIELDS AND MAE WEST
IN THE FILM MY LITTLE CHICKADEE

Starting off [a trial] with a completely open mind
is a terribly dangerous thing to do.

RT. HON. SIR MELFORD STEVENSON,
BRITISH JUDGE

Trying a case the second time is like eating
yesterday morning's oatmeal.

LLOYD PAUL STRYKER,
AMERICAN LAWYER

Trials are the most entertaining of all American
spectacles, always better than the theater,
and except for a few special cases,
much more thrilling than movies.

JOHN WATERS,
AMERICAN FILMMAKER

Can our courts remain completely independent if they
become stages for a continuing television series?
I think not. . . . Hear—but we don't need to see.

EUGENE PAVALON, PRESIDENT,
AMERICAN TRIAL LAWYERS ASSOCIATION,
ARGUING AGAINST ALLOWING CAMERAS
IN COURTROOMS

I'm worried about so much filth and indecent material
coming in through the airwaves and through these
trials into people's homes. I think the
American people have a right to be protected
against some of these excesses. While people have
a right to a fair trial, I think the American people
have an overriding right to let those matters
be decided behind closed doors.

GEORGE BUSH,
41ST PRESIDENT OF THE UNITED STATES,
REFERRING TO THE WILLIAM KENNEDY SMITH RAPE TRIAL

155

THE VERDICT

It's like seeing your mother-in-law
drive over a cliff in your new Cadillac.

DON BARRETT,
AMERICAN LAWYER,
DESCRIBING HIS REACTION WHEN
JURORS FOUND FOR HIS CLIENT BUT AWARDED
NO DAMAGES BECAUSE THEY SAID BOTH
PARTIES WERE AT FAULT

The message of the jury sent out basically is that
if you don't believe or agree with a verdict,
it is OK to go out into the streets, to choose certain
fellow human beings, throw rocks at their cars,
beat them up, and take their property.

ANONYMOUS ALTERNATE JUROR,
AFTER TWO MEN WERE ACQUITTED OF THE
MOST SERIOUS CHARGES IN THE BEATING OF
TRUCK DRIVER REGINALD DENNY DURING
THE 1992 LOS ANGELES RIOTS

I think that society is a loser in this case.
It appears now that vigilantism is not against the law,
at least in some minds. And that's a terrifying thought.

PAMELA BOZANICH,
DISTRICT ATTORNEY AND LEAD PROSECUTOR
IN THE FIRST LYLE AND ERIK MENENDEZ MURDER TRIAL

We find the defendants incredibly guilty.

FOREMAN RETURNING JURY'S VERDICT
ON MAX BIALYSTOCK AND LEO BLOOM IN
THE FILM THE PRODUCERS

157

In America, an acquittal doesn't mean you're innocent.
It means you beat the rap.
My clients lose even when they win.

F. LEE BAILEY,
AMERICAN LAWYER

When we let the victim's personal feelings
affect the judge's sentence we are reverting to a
government not of laws, but of men.

**HILLER B. ZOBEL,
AMERICAN JUDGE**

Coke and Bull Story

During an Oakland County (California) drug trial in 1990, defendant Christopher Plovic claimed that he had been searched improperly by the police. While proving his point, he handed his jacket to Judge Barry Howard.

To everyone's surprise, Judge Howard pulled out a packet of cocaine from Plovic's jacket pocket. Declared the judge, "The only thing comparable is giving a speech at your high school reunion and not realizing your zipper is down."

CLOSING ARGUMENTS

Any culture that has had its Jeffersons, Lincolns,
and Darrows also must have a
healthy notion of the lawyer's role in society.

MATTHEW A. HODEL,
AMERICAN LAWYER

Ours is a learned profession, not a mere
money-getting trade.

AMERICAN BAR ASSOCIATION COMMITTEE
ON PROFESSIONAL ETHICS AND GRIEVANCES, 1943

163

I have watched with great sadness the decline in
esteem held by our society of lawyers. There must be
a rediscovery of civility in the profession.

SANDRA DAY O'CONNOR,
SUPREME COURT JUSTICE

Those who are concerned about the public image
of our profession would do well to look at
some of this shoddy advertising.

EDWARD F. SHEA JR.,
AMERICAN LAWYER

Lawyers are given a place of privilege in this society.
They are allowed to toil in the majestic edifice
of law. This provides them with dignity, challenging
work, social power—and often an excellent income.
For those privileges, the least they can do is
behave with respect toward the institution that
gives meaning to their lives: the law.

JOSEPH A. WAPNER,
JUDGE OF THE TELEVISION SHOW
THE PEOPLE'S COURT

Any profession that suffers from so foul a reputation
must, in some way, provoke it.

ALAN DERSHOWITZ,
LAWYER AND HARVARD LAW PROFESSOR

To a large extent, lawyers have shed
traditional professional qualities, and the law
has become an ordinary trade whose success
is measured by profits.

**PETER BROWN,
AMERICAN LAWYER**

My generation and those older than I looked at law
as a profession. Too many of the younger ones
look at law as a business.

**PAMELA ANN RYMER,
LOS ANGELES FEDERAL JUDGE**

Lawyer bashing is almost as American as apple pie;
everyone knows a good lawyer joke. And for every
good lawyer joke, everyone probably knows
at least one bad lawyer.

**TODD GREER, LAW STUDENT,
UNIVERSITY OF ARKANSAS**

Lawyers as a group are no more dedicated to justice
or public service than a private public utility
is dedicated to giving light.

**DAVID MELINKOFF,
LAW PROFESSOR, UCLA**

No other profession is subject to the public contempt
and derision that sometimes befalls lawyers . . .
the bitter fruit of public incomprehension
of the law itself and its dynamics.

**IRVING R. KAUFMAN,
U.S. COURT OF APPEALS JUDGE**

Doctors . . . still retain a high degree of public
confidence because they are perceived as healers.
Should lawyers not be healers? Healers, not warriors?
Healers, not procurers? Healers, not hired guns?

**WARREN BURGER,
SUPREME COURT JUSTICE**

More Americans are terrified of being bit, bashed,
or brutalized by attorneys. No wonder they vent their
anxiety in cathartic one-liners. Should we non-lawyers
stop telling the one about the skid marks,
or the good start, or the researchers who turned to
dissecting lawyers because they got emotionally
attached to white rats?

WALTER K. OLSON,
SENIOR FELLOW, MANHATTAN INSTITUTE

It is pretty hard to find a group less concerned
with serving society and more concerned with
serving themselves than the lawyers.

FRED RODELL,
LAW PROFESSOR, YALE UNIVERSITY

Lawyers are like beavers:
they get in the mainstream and dam it up.

JOHN NAISBITT,
AMERICAN WRITER

It's not a profession at all,
but rather a business service station and repair shop.

**ADLAI E. STEVENSON,
AMERICAN LAWYER AND DIPLOMAT**

The law is the only profession which records
its mistakes carefully, exactly as they occurred,
and yet does not identify them as mistakes.

**ELLIOTT DUNLAP SMITH,
AMERICAN WRITER**

Nothing could be more boring than an absolutely
accurate movie about the law.

**ROGER EBERT,
AMERICAN FILM CRITIC**

If it's the last thing I do, I'll put you out of business.
There must be a law even for lawyers.

**LANA TURNER AS CORA SMITH,
IN THE FILM THE POSTMAN ALWAYS RINGS TWICE**

Of course had you gone to law school like
your father and I wanted you to,
your behavior would've been legal.

**MOTHER TALKING TO CONVICT SON IN JAIL,
IN CARTOONIST WILEY'S STRIP <u>NON SEQUITUR</u>**

No Respect

Public defenders don't get any respect.

While working as an assistant state's attorney in Marathon, Florida, Omar Hechavarria received a telephone call that left him scratching his head and laughing at the same time.

On the other end of the line was a woman who wanted to speak to the "public offender."

Mark A. Cooper, a public defender in Punta Gorda, Florida, was about to sign a pre-sentence investigation report when he noticed a slight mistake. The report had listed him as a "Public Defendant."

169

And Now the Good News. . . .

To help restore the poor public image of the legal profession, a Beverly Hills newspaper came up with a new feature in 1989 and asked for readers' assistance.

"We would be most grateful to receive any good news about things the lawyers have done, and we promise to print them in this new column," said the paper.

The editors waited and waited for someone, anyone, to respond. Exasperated, the paper finally squashed its own idea by running the headline, "Great Deeds by the Attorneys" over an empty space.

A is for Absurd

Everyone who has scanned the Yellow Pages knows the lengths to which businesses will go to get the first listing in their category. Attorneys have tried to get into the act too. For example:

- *A Abiding Aggressive Attorney Doug Andrews*, Savannah, Georgia
- *A Guy Who's a Lawyer*, Joseph K. Luby
- *A. Aardvark Accidents Advocacy Office of Cahen, Stephen, P.A.*, Miami
- *AAA Able And Willing Attorneys*, West Palm Beach, Florida

LEGAL FEES

A lawyer's opinion is worth nothing unless paid for.

ENGLISH PROVERB

Lawyer to potential client: You have a pretty
good case, Mr. Pitkin. How much justice
can you afford?

CARTOON CAPTION BY J.B. HANDELSMAN,
THE NEW YORKER

It is not unprofessional to give free legal advice,
but advertising that the first visit will be free is a bit like
a fox telling chickens he will not bite them until they
cross the threshold of the henhouse.

WARREN BURGER,
SUPREME COURT JUSTICE

A man may as well open an oyster without a knife,
as a lawyer's mouth without a fee.

BARTEN HOLYDAY,
17TH-CENTURY ENGLISH TRANSLATOR

A shell for thee
And a shell for thee
But the oyster is the lawyer's fee.

THOMAS LEWIS INGRAM

173

Doctors purge the body, preachers the
conscience, lawyers the purse.

GERMAN PROVERB

Do you mean to say I would be more noble
if I charged less? Where's the nobility in that?

RICHARD ISRAELS,
CANADIAN LAWYER

The public needs the equivalent of Chevrolets
as well as Cadillacs.

LEARNED HAND,
U.S. COURT OF APPEALS JUDGE,
ON THE TREND TOWARD
POPULAR MARKETING OF LEGAL SERVICES

174

I can think of no other business where you are
rewarded for inefficiency. No matter what you sell,
the fewer hours of labor that go into the product,
the more you make. With lawyers it's backwards—
the more time you take, the more inefficient
you are, the greater your profit.

ALAN LIEBOWITZ,
LAW FIRM AUDITOR

It seems for a lot of lawyers,
padding the bill is a creative challenge.

DIANE SAWYER,
AMERICAN TELEVISION JOURNALIST

Always remember that when you go
into an attorney's office, you will have to
pay for it, first or last.

ANTHONY TROLLOPE,
19TH-CENTURY ENGLISH WRITER

Lawyers charge a fortune to handle a bond offering.
You know what it takes to handle a bond offering?
The mental capabilities of a filing cabinet.

JIMMY BRESLIN,
AMERICAN WRITER

175

So St. Peter Says to the Lawyer. . . .

In a 1980 gender discrimination case involving lawyers'
fees in the District of Columbia, federal district court
judge Malcolm Wilkey told the following joke in his dissenting opinion:

"An immediately deceased lawyer arrived at the Pearly
Gates to seek admittance from St. Peter. The Keeper of

the Keys was surprisingly warm in his welcome: 'We are so glad to see you. We are particularly happy to have you here, not only because we get so few lawyers up here, but because you lived to the wonderful age of 165.' [The lawyer] was a bit doubtful and hesitant. 'Now, St. Peter, if there's one place I don't want to get into under false pretenses, it's Heaven. I really died at age 78.' St. Peter looked perplexed, frowned, and consulted the scroll in his hand. 'Ah, I see where we made our mistake as to your age. We just added up your time sheets!'"

COURTROOM PERFORMANCE

[A lawyer's] performance in the courtroom is
responsible for about 25 percent of the outcome;
the remaining 75 percent depends on the facts.

MELVIN BELLI,
AMERICAN LAWYER

Yes, there's such a thing as luck in trial law
but it only comes at 3 o'clock in the morning. . . .
You'll still find me in the library
looking for luck at 3 o'clock in the morning.

LOUIS NIZER,
AMERICAN LAWYER

A criminal lawyer, like a trapeze performer,
is seldom more than one slip from an awful fall.

PAUL O'NEIL,
AMERICAN WRITER AND JOURNALIST

Okay, it's smoke and mirrors. So what?
You'd be surprised how much of the legal process
is exactly that. Just like in Hollywood,
image is everything in the courtroom, dahhhling.

DARLENE RICKER,
AMERICAN LAWYER AND LEGAL JOURNALIST

As long as I'm in that courtroom and I feel afraid,
it means there's something in me that's contagious.
If I didn't give a damn, I wouldn't be afraid.
Fear is a wonderful emotion.

GERRY SPENCE,
AMERICAN LAWYER

The power of clear statement
is the great power at the bar.

DANIEL WEBSTER,
18TH-CENTURY AMERICAN STATESMAN,
ORATOR, AND LAWYER

One cool judgment is worth a thousand hasty counsels.
The thing to be supplied is light, not heat.

WOODROW WILSON,
28TH PRESIDENT OF THE UNITED STATES

There are times when it's not the thrill of winning.
It's the fear of losing.

ROY BLACK,
AMERICAN LAWYER

Liars are like snakes. Sooner or later
they shed their skin. The cross-examiner's job
is to make a few small incisions that will help
them do this right in front of the jury.
Cross-examination is a process in which
you loosen the witness's skin.

MIKE FICARO,
AMERICAN LAWYER

In hard-fought litigation where the stakes
are high, lawyers say and do a helluva lot of things
in anger, and only a psycho would view it as heinous!
You're not injuring anyone physically. You're not
stealing their money. What's the big problem?

MORTON GALANE,
AMERICAN LAWYER

I'm a hunter, a combatant in the courtroom.
It's just like the forest: I walk through quietly but
resolutely, ready to make a purposeful kill. You must
have great love to kill, to combat, to advocate.

GERRY SPENCE,
AMERICAN LAWYER

Trial work requires a computer mind that is rapid
in the challenge and response. It's like live TV
with no rerun. Not everyone has a mental fast ball
and those who don't shouldn't try cases.

NED GOOD,
AMERICAN LAWYER

They [prosecutors] can make Mother Theresa
look like a whore. That's what they're paid for.

LINDA COONEY,
FLORIDA HOUSEWIFE ACQUITTED OF MURDERING HER HUSBAND

Most of the great trial lawyers I know
are very, very scared. Fear, for an actor,
stirs you to a greater performance.

ARTHUR LINMAN,
AMERICAN LAWYER

181

A Sick Defense

Near the end of a lengthy bench trial in federal district court in Chicago in 1986, defense attorney William Levinson moved for a new trial—because of his own inadequate representation.

In the judge's chambers, Levinson labeled his direct examination of his client "a horror." The attorney claimed it was because he was suffering from the flu.

Presiding Judge Ann Williams denied the ill-founded motion.

THE SYSTEM

I have spent all my life under a Communist regime,
and I will tell you that a society without
any objective legal scale is a terrible one indeed.
But a society with no other scale but the legal one
is not quite worthy of man either.

ALEXANDER SOLZHENITSYN,
RUSSIAN WRITER

Adversary procedure has served as a guardian
of individual liberty since its inception.

STEPHAN LANDSMAN,
LAW PROFESSOR, MARSHALL COLLEGE

The legal system is often a mystery, and we, its priests,
preside over rituals baffling to everyday citizens.

HENRY G. MILLER,
PRESIDENT, NEW YORK STATE BAR ASSOCIATION

When Americans leave a courtroom feeling that their cries have been heard, we should all share pride in the fact that our legal system works as well as it does.

JOSEPH A. WAPNER,
JUDGE OF THE TELEVISION SHOW
THE PEOPLE'S COURT

In Germany, under the law everything is prohibited except that which is permitted. In France, under the law everything is permitted except that which is prohibited. In the Soviet Union, everything is prohibited, including that which is permitted. And in Italy, under the law everything is permitted, especially that which is prohibited.

NEWTON MINOW,
FCC CHAIRMAN AND LAWYER

183

Of course there's a different law for the rich and the poor; otherwise, who would go into business?

E. RALPH STEWART

If one man can be allowed to determine for himself
what is law, every man can. That means first chaos,
then tyranny. Legal process is an essential part
of the democratic process.

**FELIX FRANKFURTER,
SUPREME COURT JUSTICE**

The judicial system is the most expensive machine
ever invented for finding out what happened
and what to do about it.

**IRVING R. KAUFMAN,
U.S. COURT OF APPEALS JUDGE**

Before going to prison I believed that criticism of the
criminal justice system for its treatment of the poor was
so much liberal bleating and bunk. I was wrong.

**G. GORDON LIDDY,
CONVICTED NIXON PRESIDENTIAL AIDE**

This is what has to be remembered about the law:
Beneath that cold, harsh, impersonal exterior there
beats a cold, harsh, impersonal heart.

**DAVID FROST,
BRITISH TELEVISION JOURNALIST**

The law is above the law, you know.

**DOROTHY SALISBURY DAVIS,
AMERICAN WRITER**

185

If I did half of the things this sorry
President [Nixon] did, they would put me under
the jail and send every key to the moon.
They have the little punishments for the big men
and the heavy chastisement for the poor.

**RUTH SHAYS,
QUOTED IN JOHN GWALTNEY'S DRYLONGSO**

The United States is the greatest law factory
the world has ever known.

**CHARLES EVANS HUGHES,
SUPREME COURT JUSTICE**

As tort law operates now, it is more like a lottery
than like a rational system of justice.

**MICHAEL KINSLEY,
AMERICAN JOURNALIST**

Our system of civil justice is, at times,
a self-inflicted competitive disadvantage.

**J. DANFORTH QUAYLE,
44TH VICE PRESIDENT OF THE UNITED STATES**

We're doing this whole thing backward. Attorneys
should wear numbers on their backs, and box scores
should have entries for writs, dispositions, and appeals.

**BILL VEECK,
OWNER, CHICAGO WHITE SOX**

It is better to risk saving a guilty man than to
condemn an innocent one.

VOLTAIRE,
17TH-CENTURY FRENCH WRITER

People say law but they mean wealth.

RALPH WALDO EMERSON,
19TH-CENTURY AMERICAN WRITER AND POET

I use the rules to frustrate the law.
But I didn't set up the ground rules.

F. LEE BAILEY,
AMERICAN LAWYER

This case proves that our justice system works—if you
have the money and the influence to go all the way.

ROBERT ARUM,
LAWYER AND LONGTIME ASSOCIATE OF MUHAMMAD ALI,
WHEN THE SUPREME COURT REVERSED ALI'S
CONVICTION FOR DRAFT EVASION

There is far too much law for those who can afford it
and far too little for those who cannot.

DEREK C. BOK,
PRESIDENT, HARVARD UNIVERSITY

In law, nothing is certain but the expense.

SAMUEL BUTLER,
17TH-CENTURY ENGLISH WRITER

188

Laws grind the poor, and rich men rule the law.

OLIVER GOLDSMITH,
18TH-CENTURY ENGLISH WRITER

A poor man may still be able to get into heaven,
but after Reaganization,
he may not be able to get into court.

JANE BRYANT QUINN,
AMERICAN JOURNALIST

An incompetent attorney can delay a trial
for years or months. A competent attorney
can delay one even longer.

EVELLE J. YOUNGER,
AMERICAN LAWYER

America is the paradise of lawyers.

DAVID J. BREWER,
SUPREME COURT JUSTICE

189

Woman was and is condemned to a system
under which the lawful rapes exceed
the unlawful ones a million to one.

MARGARET SANGER,
AMERICAN POLITICAL ACTIVIST

Law is a reflection and a source of prejudice.
It both enforces and suggests forms of bias.

DIANE B. SCHULDER,
AMERICAN LAWYER AND EDUCATOR

I wept for this little girl's lost childhood.
I wept for Thomas Jefferson, George Washington,
John Adams and all of our brave forefathers. . . .
And most of all, I wept for the fact that our laws have
become an object of disrespect, a paper tiger that no
longer insures or gives adequate redress to the most ele-
mental right of all to live in peace and relative freedom
from fear of those who would violate those laws.

EDWARD A. MILLER, FLORIDA JUDGE,
AFTER BEING FORCED BY LAW
TO REDUCE A RAPIST'S SENTENCE IN 1993

The plain truth of the matter is that rather than
alter a system that has now proven without a doubt
to be incapable of dealing with crime, our society has
altered itself and ignored the problem by sticking
our heads in the sand like the proverbial ostrich
until he wound up in the belly of a lion.

EDWARD A. MILLER, FLORIDA JUDGE,
IN A 1993 LETTER TO THE EDITOR WHICH LED
TO A REPRIMAND FROM THE FLORIDA SUPREME COURT

It isn't the bad lawyers who are screwing up
the justice system in this country, it's the good lawyers.
If you have two competent lawyers on opposite sides,
a trial that should take three days could
easily last six months.

**ART BUCHWALD,
AMERICAN JOURNALIST**

Ours is a prostitute society. The system of justice,
and most especially the legal profession, is a whorehouse
serving those best able to afford the luxuries of justice
offered to preferred customers. The lawyer, in these
terms, is analogous to a prostitute. The difference
between the two is simple. The prostitute is honest—the
buck is her aim. The lawyer is dishonest—he claims that
justice, service to mankind is his primary purpose.
The lawyer's deception of the people springs from his
actual money-making role; he represents the client
who puts the highest fee on the table.

**FLORYNCE RAE KENNEDY,
AMERICAN LAWYER AND CIVIL RIGHTS ACTIVIST**

Justice is a system of revenge wherein
the State imitates the criminal.

ELBERT HUBBARD,
AMERICAN WRITER AND EDITOR

To be a trial lawyer is to see the ignominy of slow
justice in a system in which the process itself
punishes all who come in contact with it—
the winner as well as the loser.

JOHN A. JENKINS,
JOURNALIST AND LEGAL WRITER

I cannot believe that a republic could hope to exist
at the present time, if the influence of lawyers in
public business did not increase in proportion
to the power of the people.

ALEXIS DE TOCQUEVILLE,
19TH-CENTURY FRENCH STATESMAN AND WRITER

We've produced a system of ending disputes
rather than digging up truths.

THOMAS H. ALLEN,
AMERICAN LAWYER

By the argument of counsel it was shown that
at half-past ten in the morning on the day of the
murder, . . . [the defendant] became insane,
and remained so for eleven hours and a half exactly.

MARK TWAIN,
AMERICAN WRITER AND HUMORIST,
COMMENTING ON THE INSANITY DEFENSE

I think the law became an ass the day it let
the psychiatrists get their hands on it.

LYNN COMPTON,
LOS ANGELES CHIEF DEPUTY DISTRICT ATTORNEY,
AT THE SUMMATION OF SIRHAN SIRHAN'S TRIAL
FOR ASSASSINATING ROBERT F. KENNEDY

> An appeal, Hinnissy, is where ye ask wan coort
> to show its contempt f'r another coort.
>
> **MR. DOOLEY [FINLEY PETER DUNNE],**
> **AMERICAN HUMORIST**

Sock it to Him

When Ed Koch was running for mayor in New York City in 1973, he went to a senior citizens center in the Bronx.

The candidate was immediately asked about crime and what he intended to do about it. "Crime is terrible," he replied. "A judge I know was mugged this week and do you know what he did? He called a press conference and said the mugging would in no way affect his judicial decisions in matters of that kind."

An elderly woman stood up and shouted, "Then mug him again!"

A Ruling that Made No Cents

After four years of legal wranglings over the ownership of some property in Palmdale, California, a settlement was finally reached in 1992—but justice was held up over a single penny.

L.A. Superior Court officials refused to let the two parties split a $30,832.81 deposit because one party would receive a penny more than the other. Attorneys from both sides offered to toss in a cent to make it even, but the officials insisted on a new formal order.

To satisfy the court finance officer, a new court order was drawn up and sent by messenger to all parties who had to appear at an early-morning special court hearing. The legal costs to resolve the one-cent issue: $1,050.

Three Tiers for the Judge

Before three justices in the Hong Kong Court of Criminal Appeals, lawyer Angus McKay gave three reasons why he felt his client's conviction should be overturned.

"Mr. McKay," said one of the judges, "the first tier of your case is that the identification was wrong, the second tier that the statements should have been disregarded, and the third tier is that the conviction is against the weight of evidence in any event, is that not right?"

McKay couldn't resist a clever reply: "If I have reduced your Lordship to tiers, should I really continue?"

Typos

A 1991 brief said it had an index containing an "extensive copulation of authorities."

• A 1992 court paper was addressed to "The Horable U.S. District Judge."

• A 1993 notice of appeal ended with "Rectfully submitted."

• A 1993 agricultural lease involving demised premises stated the tenant was entitled to exclusive use and possession of the "demised penises."

• A 1990 estate plan attempted a distribution of "asses."

O N   R E F O R M

Even when laws have been written down, they ought
not always to remain unaltered.

ARISTOTLE,
4TH-CENTURY B.C. GREEK PHILOSOPHER

Law is merely the expression of the will of the strongest
for the time being, and therefore laws have no fixity,
but shift from generation to generation.

BROOKS ADAMS,
19TH-CENTURY AMERICAN HISTORIAN

The law, like the traveler, must be ready
for the morrow. It must have the principle of growth.

BENJAMIN CARDOZO,
SUPREME COURT JUSTICE

To the law we bow with reverence. It is the one king
that commands our allegiance. We will change
our king when his rule is oppressive.

BENJAMIN HARRISON,
23RD PRESIDENT OF THE UNITED STATES

Nothing is more subject to change than the laws.

MICHEL DE MONTAIGNE,
16TH-CENTURY FRENCH WRITER

Laws should not be changed without good reason.

CHARLES LOUIS DE MONTESQUIEU,
17TH-CENTURY FRENCH LAWYER AND
POLITICAL PHILOSOPHER

When I hear any man talk of an unalterable law,
the only effect it produces upon me is to convince me
that he is an unalterable fool.

SYDNEY SMITH,
18TH-CENTURY ENGLISH WRITER

Somewhere "out there," beyond the walls of the
courthouse, run currents and tides of public opinion
which lap at the courtroom door.

WILLIAM H. REHNQUIST,
SUPREME COURT JUSTICE, ON THE PUBLIC'S
INFLUENCE TO CHANGE LAWS

Law reform is far too serious a matter
to be left to the legal profession.

LORD LESLIE SCARMAN,
ENGLISH LAWYER

199

If you got the sayso you want to keep it,
whether you are right or wrong. That's why they have
to keep changing the laws—so they don't unbenefit
any of these big white men.

RUTH SHAYS,
QUOTED IN JOHN GWALTNEY'S DRYLONGSO

Law and justice are not always the same.
When they aren't, destroying the law may be
the first step toward changing it.

GLORIA STEINEM,
AMERICAN WRITER AND FEMINIST

We have the means to change the laws we find unjust
or onerous. We cannot, as citizens, pick and choose the
laws we will or will not obey.

RONALD W. REAGAN,
40TH PRESIDENT OF THE UNITED STATES

Laws and institutions are constantly tending
to gravitate. Like clocks, they must be occasionally
cleansed, and wound up, and set to true time.

HENRY WARD BEECHER,
19TH-CENTURY AMERICAN CLERGYMAN

Law and equity are two things that God hath joined,
but which man hath put asunder.

CHARLES C. COLTON,
18TH-CENTURY ENGLISH CLERGYMAN AND WRITER

The worse the society, the more law there will be.
In Hell there will be nothing but law, and due process
will be meticulously observed.

GRANT GILMORE,
LEGAL SCHOLAR

The rule of law can be wiped out in one misguided,
however well-intentioned, generation.

WILLIAM T. GOSSETT,
PRESIDENT, AMERICAN BAR ASSOCIATION

New lords, new laws.

SIR JOHN HARINGTON,
16TH-CENTURY ENGLISH WRITER AND TRANSLATOR

It cannot be helped, it is as it should be,
that the law is behind the times.

OLIVER WENDELL HOLMES JR.,
SUPREME COURT JUSTICE

Law must be stable and yet it cannot stand still.

ROSCOE POUND,
DEAN EMERITUS, HARVARD LAW SCHOOL

202

Petty laws breed great crimes.

OUIDA,
18TH-CENTURY SCOTTISH WRITER

The law changes and flows like water, and . . .
the stream of women's rights law has become
a sudden rushing torrent.

SHANA ALEXANDER,
AMERICAN JOURNALIST

It is perfectly proper to regard and study the law
simply as a great anthropological document.

OLIVER WENDELL HOLMES JR.,
SUPREME COURT JUSTICE

Every new time will give its law.

MAXIM GORKY,
RUSSIAN WRITER

Legaldegook

Here are some 1993 winners of the annual Legal-
degook Awards, selected by the Plain Language
Committee of the State Bar of Texas:

• To an attorney who claims his position is supported
by a statement in an accompanying affidavit in the case
file: "It all fully appears from the affidavit of the publisher heretofore herein filed."

• To an attorney who writes that the pleading may
refer to other documents previously filed: "The Court

may take judicial notice of such pleadings which are on file herein and such pleadings are incorporated herein by reference and made a part hereof as if copied here in full."

Who Do You Trust?

When Miami lawyer Stephen Nagin received a call one day in 1991 from a potential client who wanted a divorce, he was perplexed because he specialized in antitrust suits.

"Why would you call me?" he asked the woman caller.

"Well," she replied, "I saw your name in the Yellow Pages under antitrust lawyers, and I don't trust my husband."

Nagin respectfully declined to represent her.

A D V I C E   T O   L A W Y E R S

I'll tell you what my daddy told me after my first trial.
I thought I was just great. I asked him, "How did I do?"
He paused and said, "You've got to guard against
speaking more clearly than you think."

HOWARD H. BAKER JR.,
UNITED STATES SENATOR

205

You don't approach a case with the philosophy of
applying abstract justice—you go in to win.

PERCY FOREMAN,
AMERICAN LAWYER

Be concise for clients. Less is more.
Bravura displays only serve to irritate;
brevity is what pays the rent.

JAMES C. FREUND,
AMERICAN LAWYER

Be you never so high, the law is above you.

THOMAS FULLER,
17TH-CENTURY ENGLISH WRITER

When you have the facts on your side,
argue the facts. When you have the law on your side,
argue the law. When you have neither, holler.

ALBERT GORE JR.,
45TH VICE PRESIDENT OF THE UNITED STATES

When you have no basis for an argument,
abuse the plaintiff.

CICERO,
1ST-CENTURY B.C. ROMAN STATESMAN,
ORATOR, AND WRITER

My thesis is that the truly successful lawyer
finds a good heart more useful than sharp fangs.

MATTHEW A. HODEL,
AMERICAN LAWYER

There is a vague popular belief that lawyers are necessarily dishonest. I say vague, because when we consider to what extent confidence and honors are reposed in and conferred upon lawyers by the people, it appears improbable that their impression of dishonesty is very distinct and vivid. Yet the impression is common, almost universal. Let no young man choosing the law for a calling for a moment yield to the popular belief—resolve to be honest at all events; and if in your own judgment you cannot be an honest lawyer, resolve to be honest without being a lawyer. Choose some other occupation, rather than one in the choosing of which you do, in advance, consent to be a knave.

ABRAHAM LINCOLN,
16TH PRESIDENT OF THE UNITED STATES

In university they don't tell you that the greater part of the law is learning to tolerate fools.

DORIS LESSING,
ENGLISH WRITER

I used to say that, as Solicitor General,
I made three arguments of every case.
First came the one that I planned as I thought—
logical, coherent, complete. Second was the one
actually presented—interrupted, incoherent,
disjointed, disappointing. The third was
the utterly devastating argument that I thought
of after going to bed that night.

**ROBERT H. JACKSON,
SUPREME COURT JUSTICE**

208

Never, never, never, on cross examination,
ask a witness a question you don't already
know the answer to, was a tenet I absorbed with
my baby food. Do it, and you'll often get
an answer you don't want.

**ATTICUS FINCH
IN HARPER LEE'S TO KILL A MOCKINGBIRD**

[Preparation] is the be-all of good trial work.
Everything else—felicity of expression, improvisational
brilliance—is a satellite around the sun.
Thorough preparation is that sun.

LOUIS NIZER,
AMERICAN LAWYER

People don't ordinarily look forward to starting at
the bottom. While you may be a lowly foot soldier . . .
no one knows more about solving a problem
than the person at the bottom.

SANDRA DAY O'CONNOR,
SUPREME COURT JUSTICE,
RECALLING THE DAYS EARLY IN HER CAREER
IN A MALL LAW OFFICE COLLECTING
UNPAID GROCERY BILLS

209

There is always room at the top.

DANIEL WEBSTER,
AMERICAN STATESMAN, ORATOR, AND LAWYER,
WHEN ADVISED NOT TO BECOME
A LAWYER BECAUSE THE PROFESSION
WAS OVERCROWDED

Extemporaneous speaking should be practiced
and cultivated. It is the lawyer's avenue to the public.

ABRAHAM LINCOLN,
16TH PRESIDENT OF THE UNITED STATES

Wisdom too often never comes, and so one ought not
to reject it merely because it comes too late.

FELIX FRANKFURTER,
SUPREME COURT JUSTICE

My father told me that all you need to succeed
in the law is a certain amount of
common sense and clean fingernails.

JOHN MORTIMER,
ENGLISH LAWYER AND WRITER

Court in Repose

After a big lunch one day in 1989, Judge George D. Warner Jr. of the Chancery Court in Meridian, Mississippi, couldn't keep his eyes open in court. He realized he had dropped off to sleep when he cracked his eyes open and not a sound could be heard.

One lawyer was looking at him with his notes in his hand. The other lawyer questioning the witness was standing still before proceeding.

Judge Warner looked at the first lawyer and announced, "Objection sustained!"

"But, Judge, I didn't object," the lawyer said.

"Well," said the embarrassed judge, "you should have!"

Coup de Cliche

During a long and acrimonious 1991 trial, Judge R. William Schoettler of the Los Angeles Superior Court attempted to get the defendant's lawyer to re-phrase a question to get around an objection.

The lawyer balked at using the judge's wording and the objection stood. "Well," said the judge, "you can lead a horse to water. . . ."

The plaintiff's counsel interrupted, "You've got the wrong end, your honor."

Bruce Nash and Allan Zullo have co-authored more than sixty books together, including the best-selling Sports Hall of Shame and Amazing But True series. Bruce lives with his family in Los Angeles where he produces and writes television programs. Allan writes adult and children's books and lives in Palm Beach Gardens, Florida, with his wife, collaborator Kathryn Zullo, a freelance researcher.